Dear Anne,

Every good wish today
and always. Thank you for
all your support + kindness.

Niamh x

The human in the Universe

GW00671589

By

Niamh Brennan

To my grandmother, Nora Kelly

and to my parents,

Jim and Sheila Brennan

The human in the Universe
by Niamh Brennan
Copyright © 2014 Niamh Brennan

Library of Congress
LOC 2014956950
ISBN 978-155605-460-0

EBook Version 978-155605-461-7

Wyndham Hall Press
5050 Kerr Rd.
Lima, OH 45806
www.wyndhamhallpress.com

Acknowledgements

There are so many people that have contributed to this book, from Vinnie Busch who handed me Thomas Berry and Brian Swimme's book 'The Universe Story' on a wet and humid day in the Philippines in 2006, urging me to read it immediately; to Mary Teresa McCormack who urged me to take a step further and go to the Sophia Centre in California to study; to Jim Conlon, Director of the Sophia Center who opened up a whole new world of hope and possibility and joy to me. His influence, in my thought and in my life, has been immense. To all the wonderful people I met while there – Brian Swimme, Miriam MacGillis, Mary Schmidt, Judy Cauley, Youngmin Song, Kay Burrough, Tony Hempenstall, Gloria Canama. Wonderful people who believe the world can be bettered, who believe we can be bettered.

To the Society of St. Columban, another defining influence on my thought and life.

There are others too, whom without their support, this book would never have come to fruition. Thank you for your belief and for taking the chance.

Thanks too to all at Wyndham Hall Press, especially Mark, and to Eilish Dillon and Juliet Carey who went through the manuscript for me.

And finally, thanks to my family and friends for their support and encouragement.

Much love and gratitude, x

CONTENTS

Chapter 1
Introduction

As a species, we have walked on this Earth for over two million years, very new arrivals in the history of the cosmos. We have passed through many forms and ways of being, from Homo habilis, to Homo erectus to our current incarnation as Homo sapiens sapiens 'the one who knows they know'. In our short time here, we have come to dominate the planet like no other species ever has, becoming a presence that not only determines the future of other species but also, the future of the planet itself. And yet, as we march on in the midst of our dubious conquest, the essence of what we are and why we might be here remains a question that we still struggle to answer.

It seems that the human is fated to grapple with such questions, the existential questions that have plagued the minds of philosophers, theologians, artists, poets and scientists, of any thinking person. We have asked these questions individually – who am I? Why am I here? Do I matter? And collectively - what is the essence of our nature and the nature of our desires? Why do we act the way we do? What is consciousness? And yet we are still unsure of what it means to be called human. We still struggle to understand the significance of what it is to be the Earth in thought as it walks upon itself, to be the star at night as it gazes upon itself, to be so profoundly self-destructive and so unceasingly aspiring.

It could be argued that in the past fifty years, these bigger questions have taken a back seat and the search for meaning is no longer encouraged. But to ask these questions is natural to us. It is a consequence of being conscious and these questions are as old as humanity itself.

Time and time throughout history we have had to refine, adjust and even discard the worldview that gave meaning to our existence as we began to learn more of the Universe that holds us. In the words of Carl Sagan:

> ...*in the last tenth of a percent of the lifetime of our species, in the instant between Aristarchus and ourselves, we reluctantly noticed that we were not the center and purpose of the Universe, but rather lived on a tiny and fragile world lost in immensity and eternity, drifting in a great cosmic ocean dotted here and there with a hundred billion galaxies and a billion trillion stars.*[1]

The assimilation of this information required a shift in consciousness about who we were within this immense reality. With contemporary science, our knowledge of the Universe has continued to grow so that a further shift is needed. It is no longer viable to view the human as the pinnacle of creation. It is equally no longer viable to view the Universe as static and unchanging. We now know that we live in a Universe that continues both to expand and to evolve. What does this mean for such anthropocentric questions as 'who am I?' and indeed for the species who has uncovered such things?

Cultural Historian, Thomas Berry has written that we do not know where we are in time and space except for the story of events that have taken place. Thanks to the observational sciences we now have access to this story of events as represented and described in the story of the Universe. This is the story of our origins gained through modern scientific insight and it describes the evolution of developmental time from the primordial flaring forth some 13.8 billion years ago, as far as and encapsulating the birth of consciousness in the human being. It describes the processes which gave rise to Earth, the evolution of life on Earth and within it, the emergence of the human species. It contextualises the human story within the larger cosmic story.

Since I began to hear this story of the Universe, to let it sink into me, something resonated with me on a level that was both deeper than previous experience and also extremely familiar. This story went to my bones. It was written in my cells and my DNA and in the very way that I understood the world. A world that was saturated with the divine, an Earth as sacred as the bible, the Universe to quote Thomas Berry, as primary revelation. I felt this story as a gift that opened my eyes and cleansed my heart, letting me breathe again, letting me know and feel and be overwhelmed by gratitude for my shaky and nebulous existence, giving me gravity and affirming everything that lived and had ever lived. A gift that made me stop and listen to birds as they sang; that made me notice the way the trees bent in the wind, that made me bend down to smell flowers and wonder about the journey they had made from the darkness of the soil until they blossomed under the sun, that made me get lost in watching ants walk their brave and laborious trail, that made me bow before the hummingbird, the most beautiful creature I have ever seen. It was as if I had been lifted out of my own insular existence and shown life for the first time, the entire myriad of life, bustling and busy and beautiful, going on its way, splendidly, sacredly.

I wondered why this information affected me so and if it could produce such freedom and gratitude in me, might it do the same for others? I thought back to Thomas Berry's words and the importance of knowing our story and realised that this Universe story *is* our story, and we learn from it that as the mysteries of the Universe are slowly revealing themselves to the human that the Universe is also revealing itself through the human. There is no distinction, no line or boundary between what it means to be the Universe and what it means to be human. Both are different expressions of the same thing, both bound up with the other - and this is what humanity is, the Universe come to thought. But it's not just humanity, the whole world speaks and breathes and participates in this ancient story, each being in its own inimitable way. As the human element, we too, participate in this story but with this new knowledge, we can now be informed about how best to participate, about the choices we make, the qualities we value and the kind of future we wish to create.

This information is a gift. It is a gift to a humanity that struggles in their sense of self, in their sense of belonging, in their very existence. It holds implications for how we see ourselves and how we live our lives, implications for all those particularities that make up a human life - love and consciousness, friendship and joy and suffering. The story of the Universe calls us to re-examine who we are within this great unfolding. It demands that we do so, demands that we ask those questions again.

And so in this book, this is what I have tried to do. It was undertaken in the assumption that if we had a greater understanding of where we come from then we would have a greater understanding of who we are. It was also undertaken in the hope that the same joy might be released in others as was released in me when I first learned this story. It has come from an examination of my own experiences in the hope that what is personal to me might also relate to the universal, from the assumption that my own nature is reflective of and an example of human nature in general. It is a case study of myself so to speak, from my own questions and for my own clarity, in light of what I know and am learning of this Universe story. Thomas Berry has written that the very role that is unique to our human species is to reflect on the deepest mysteries of the Universe and to celebrate these mysteries through our capacity of conscious self-awareness. I have taken him at his word. These are my thoughts.

Chapter 2
What Do We Know?
....A Brief Cosmic History

For the first time in history, we stand in the unique position of being able to speak with some accuracy and information about the Universe. We know, through physics and chemistry and the dedicated minds of persistent and curious individuals, a great deal about how the Universe works, how old it is and what it is composed of. What we do not know is most likely immense and inconceivable, what remains to be discovered, limitless. But what we have already learned changes the very nature of what it means to be here and of what it means to be human.

In the past five hundred years, science has slowly been piecing together the structures, processes and evolution of the Universe. What is emerging from this mammoth task is the wondrous story of our origins and of the origin of all beings. We are the generation who now know enough to be able to talk about the Universe in which we live, to be able to describe it and explain certain aspects of its behaviour.

So what do we know? I am grateful in this section for the knowledge and work of people such as Brian Swimme, Thomas Berry, Larry Edwards, Richard Fortey, Richard Dawkins, Todd Duncan, E.O. Wilson, Greg Morter and others who have helped to piece this story together.

Galactic Phase

I am not a scientist. My understanding of this story is basic and simple. I can grasp the concepts and main ideas but the details elude me. Still, I have found that the concepts are enough to move me and to make me want to learn more. I have learned that at one time, there was nothing, no 'thing' at all. That in itself is enough to ponder on for the rest of one's life and which some of the greatest minds who are bringing us this story did, people like the German philosopher, Martin Heidegger who posed the question of why there was something instead of nothing. But difficult as it is to take in, it seems that there really was a beginning to this great adventure. Some people call this beginning the Big Bang, others call it the primordial Flaring Forth. Regardless of name, it was the event when light and matter burst forth, and time and energy were created, and is estimated to have occurred roughly 13.8 billion years ago.

We now know that the entire Universe began as a single point the size of a pinprick that was trillions of degrees hot and instantly rushed apart creating and expanding space. We can see the elegance and precision at work in the Universe in this expansion alone. If the Universe had expanded one millionth of a percent slower than it had, it would have collapsed. If it had expanded one millionth of a percent faster, it would have been too quick for structures to form and would have diffused into dust. Its unfurling was so utterly exact.

As it cooled down, some half a billion years later, the particles bonded together to form the first atoms of hydrogen and helium and lithium. These atoms then began to clump into clouds of gases which collapsed into billions and billions of blazing stars and formed galaxies lighting up the sky and clearing the dusty fog of atoms making the Universe transparent as it is today. Through supernova explosions, the elements that were being cooked up in the stars were spread throughout the galaxies. Within a billion years the Universe had formed 100 billion galaxies, one of which was our own galaxy, the Milky Way.

Then, 4.6 billion years ago, three supernova explosions in the Orion arm of the Milky Way, our galactic home, triggered more star formations and our sun was born. From the remnants of the clouds of dust of hydrogen, carbon, silicon and other elements circling this new star, our solar system with its eight planets, including Earth, was also born. This process, the formation of Earth, took the lengthy time of approximately 9 billion years. It could not have happened without first the creation of stars and second the death of stars. Earth is formed from all those elements that were previously spilled across space in supernova explosions. We, the human being and every other being on Earth, are also made up of these elements. With the exception of hydrogen, every atom in our body was formed in the stars, every atom of iron in our body was once in the core of a star; stars who lived and died even before our own star, the sun was born. In the words of Brian Swimme and Mary Evelyn Tucker, and in a most factual way – *"The stars are our ancestors. Out of them everything comes forth."*[1]

Earth Phase

Some nine billion years after the initial Flaring Forth, composed of the elements created by the stars, our Earth began to develop. It is difficult to imagine that Earth was not always as she is now bustling with sound and colour, with the music of the birds and the scent of the roses, decorated with woodlands and rivers and brimming with every variety of life. It is equally difficult to imagine that she will not remain this way and strangely frightening to think that we cannot say with accuracy what may happen to her, but we can see that there is one constant in this Universe and that is transformation and change. Matter changes form. Who knows what that means for this planet?

In its early stages Earth was wild and frenzied trying to balance between rigid rock and gas. One of the images used for early Earth is that of Dante's Hell, another is of a fiery cauldron, boiling and bubbling with its elements moving between gaseous, solid and liquid states. For several million years Earth was pounded by meteorites and collided with planetoids, one of which sent large portions of Earth blasting into space. This eventually stabilised and froze to become our moon. The heavier metals such as iron and nickel sank to Earth's core with the lighter elements piling on top of these and forming the mantle. Lastly, Earth's crust formed around the mantle. Gigantic electrical storms raged down on Earth and huge volcanic eruptions occurred on her surface creating the early mountains and continents.

Over time Earth began to cool and as it did it rained. It rained for thousands and thousands of years. The rain pounded down on the rock until the seas rose up and surrounded the young mountains. The sea spread over the land covering most of its surface. Our planet was now a planet of land and water and atmosphere.

Although at ninety three million miles away we only receive a very tiny sliver of the sun's energy, it is because of this that Earth, within this solar system, was the only planet to produce complex life. We live in what is known as the habitable zone and our planet is exactly the right distance from the sun and exactly the right size for life to come forth. The bigger planets in the Solar System remained planets of gas (Jupiter, Saturn, Neptune and Uranus), and the smaller planets cooled into rock (Mercury, Venus, Mars). Earth was a mixture of both.

Earth grew into the planet it is today, the planet that is home to us and an estimated eight billion other species. For every human standing on the Earth right now, there is an entire corresponding species! After billions of years of development Earth became a planet surrounded by a thin layer of atmosphere with great circling oceans and looming mountains and the conditions right for life to come forth. And 3.8 billion years ago, life did come forth. Lightning struck the sea creating a chemical reaction and life was born in the oceans.

Life

The story of life on Earth is a story that is beyond my capability to tell. I read about evolution and the creative ways that life has evolved starting from one single cell into the body that is my own and all the other people I share the planet with as well as the animals and birds and plants, and I continue to be amazed. It is the story of our connection and relatedness, of how life has continued to develop into ever more complex ways of being. Evolutionary biologist, Richard Dawkins writes that the story of evolution when told forwards, is a story of diversity and when told backwards is a story of unity. I particularly like Palaeontologist Richard Fortey's analogy to Life. He writes:

> *I think of Maurice Ravel's dance, Bolero, which starts slowly, uneventfully, a long series of slight variations upon a recurrent theme, gradually gathering pace, shifting from one instrument to another, while an underlying pulse goes on and on. From time to time there are shifts in key, then more instruments join in, and the pace and excitement build, until, at the end, it is a scurrying, swirling mass of interwoven instrumental activity.*[2]

Others have used the term 'nesting' to describe life and how it has developed. To use Rupert Sheldrake's example "*societies of organisms contain animals, which contain organs, which contain tissues, which contain cells, which contain molecules, which contain atoms*" [3] although you could say it happened the other way around. Life keeps what works and passes it on, such examples being the eye and the lung, the brain. The first simple cells appeared roughly 3.8 billion years ago in the deep sea vents of the oceans. These were bacteria and are still in existence today. Although the 'simplest' of life forms in their make-up, it was these first cells that invented photosynthesis and so ensured that life could continue and flourish. The Trilobite who lived some five hundred million years ago invented the first eye. The Trilobite is now extinct, the 'eye' however, continues.

From these single cells more complex cells began to develop. Over time cells paired off and fused into entirely new beings marking the beginning of sexual reproduction and a bursting forth of diversity. And so it goes on, from the first jawed fish 425 million years ago to the development of the fin. From insects to the first lung which was also developed in a fish, to the first reptiles 313 million years ago to mammals 210 million years ago and the first human only 2.6 million years ago. Each species shaped by and adapting to its environment, the coat of the polar bear; the speed of the panther; the Emergent trees of the rainforest, the horns of the bison, the beak of the woodpecker. The essence of life is relationship, each being dependent on and involved in the evolution of the other.

American Naturalist John Muir once wrote "When we try to pick out anything by itself, we find it hitched to everything else in the Universe." And so it is on Earth. Think of our atmosphere which is 21% oxygen. This atmosphere of oxygen was created. Initially, oxygen was mostly locked into rocks and soil but was slowly released into the air by plants, making animal life possible. (An interesting aside and example of self-organising systems which was provided in the book, 'The Journey of the Universe' – the sun has increased in temperature by 25% in the past 4 billion years and yet the surface temperature of Earth has remained the same, adapting and organising to remain in that thin stratum that enables life to flourish.) Think of our forests, which not only are a home to thousands of species but also store carbon and stabilise our climate. Think of our oceans, home to 10% of all known animal species but also playing a vital role in soaking up excess heat in the atmosphere and distributing it more evenly around Earth. Think of insects, not only for their role in pollination but also for the role they play in decomposition, nutrient and energy recycling and soil aeration. Life is a web with each being sewn in and playing their part. It works, in the words of James Lovelock, because it works together. One living system, a whole, a whole that is nested within a solar system, nested within a galaxy, nested within the Universe.

The development of life is also the story of ever increasing complexity. This has reached a new stage in the human, that species in whom the Universe has come to conscious self-awareness.

The Human

The human, so they say, arrived quietly. A courageous and curious group of chimplike apes left the forests to search for food supplies that were becoming scarce. To do this they ventured out into the open savannahs of central Africa. It was around this time that they began to stand on two feet, a trait known as bipedalism. There are many theories as to why this happened, one being that it freed the hands to carry food.

It was also around this time that the brain began to significantly enlarge. Some scientists suggest that this inflation was due to the freeing of the hands and the opportunity this gave to using our hands for precision oriented and controlled tasks such as tool making. Over time and with the curiosity (as well as necessity) that defines our species and perhaps life itself, the human spread across the globe becoming a planetary presence.

As we have grown as a species and increased in population and knowledge, our way of organising ourselves has also changed. We have spent our longest period in the Paleolithic era as hunter-gatherers. This was the time from 2.6 million years ago to circa 12,000 BCE. It was the time when we made our most significant discoveries and advances, advances which would instigate the phenomena of cultural evolution and the human colonisation of Earth. Among these advances were the controlled use of fire, tool-making, ritual burial, art and language. With these advancements mastered and incorporated into daily human behaviour, the human entered into its next phase, the Neolithic era.

During this period which lasted roughly from 12,000 BCE to 3500 BCE, equipped with 2 million years of innovation and adaptations, the human began to tame animals and cultivate the land. This in turn led to agriculture. It meant that the human no longer needed to roam in search of food but could live their whole life in the same settlement, certain of food and certain of shelter. As a result of this, larger and larger settlements were constructed, villages initially, then towns and then cities. The human eventually entered the phase of the great classical civilisations and with them came religious ritual and ceremony, politics and government, architecture and literature. During this time, both the wheel and writing were invented. Both of these would have huge consequences for the future of humanity. With the wheel came the beginning of machinery and technology and with writing came the beginning of a stored mind that eventually every human might have access to.

And so, our development and innovations began to accelerate and we witnessed the building of ships and the beginning of colonisation and global travel, the rise of nations, the invention of the motorcar, television, telephones, space travel, the internet, and a ballooning human population. All these 'achievements', all these 'advancements' are so bound into the fabric of our life now, particularly in the global North, that we take them for granted and have become largely immune to them. We use them without hardly a thought. They have become extensions of the human, the means through which we act.

But in spite of all these developments, this is where we, the Homo sapiens, are now - a population of 7 billion people where 8.5% of the population own 83.4% of all household wealth; where 21,000 people, mostly children, die of hunger every day; where over half a million people are murdered each year and where there are at present an estimated twenty-seven on-going armed conflicts taking place.

But these are the externalities of our story, this is the history of the outside, the 'what happened' in a time linear, chronological scale. It shows us the power of our species and what we are capable of doing. A young species with an unparalleled curiosity, an enormous brain with which to satiate this curiosity and the power of thought which fuels both. But what do these achievements reveal about us? What does it mean that we can leave our planet and walk on the moon, look back and capture time in a photograph of Earth? What kind of a creature are we that we can do this and what is its relation to the Universe?

Chapter 3
Principles of the Universe

Before we begin to explore the human and examine what our role may be here if indeed we have one, we must first look at some of the laws that appear to be present within the Universe, as such laws will have an impact in how the human unfolds. Thomas Berry, geologian and academic, was one of the leading proponents of this story. He wrote that there are certain principles or laws that are evident within our Universe, a principle being such that it is a rule or standard that is contained within the process and functioning of the Universe. These principles or laws are active at all levels of reality from the macro-cosmos to the micro-cosmos and as such their presence is particularly valid for what it teaches us about how the Universe works. In this chapter I will look at some of these principles but first I will begin with two challenging facts.

One Source

While not a principle or law, this fact is significant enough to be reflected on and what it may mean in detail, and where better to start than the beginning? Science teaches us that everything that ever was and that will ever be, was contained in that fireball which burst into existence so splendidly and so mysteriously some 13.8 billion years ago. The origin of all things from one source. A source whose existence itself is inexplicable, shrouded in a mystery that the human has not yet been able to penetrate. A source that is becoming physically more expressed as time passes, making explicit that which has been implicit since the beginning. Quantum physicist David Bohm articulates how this present moment is the explicate form of the origin moment. Just as the present moment was implicitly present at the beginning before it was expressed and made explicit, so too is the origin moment present implicitly now. This, the 'implicate order' is not composed of matter but has the power to generate matter and any particle that emerges from the implicate order remains in connection with this hidden realm of the Universe and with that first moment.

So what is the significance of coming from only one source? It means that connection and relationship are fundamental to our existence. Not only do we have a common ancestor but we have a shared beginning making us different expressions of the same thing, making us One. Think of the seed of the pansy flower, planted in early spring that begins to bloom in summer, its slight, green stem and leaves complimented by an assortment of flowers of white, purple and yellow, each expressing something specific of the nature of the pansy but all coming from the same seed, all the one plant. So it is with this Universe, it takes its expression in different forms. The Universe in the form of a galaxy; the Universe in the form of Earth; the Universe in the form of a pansy, the Universe in the form of me. A common energy travelling through time expressing itself differently but equally present in each form. This ancient source, that philosopher Jean Gebser beautifully named the Ever Present Origin is the energy that permeates the world.

For many centuries, the concepts of separation, isolation and aloneness have occupied the thoughts of our post-industrialist mind. The more we have developed our thinking, the more we have been able to objectify ourselves and to think of ourselves as separate beings. This has created a sense of loneliness which now seems part of the human condition. And yet this new information from science is telling us that separation is an illusion, as is isolation, so why do we indulge them? We are all, in a particular form, a result of that initial flaring forth, sharing that same energy, that same divine spark of life. We share, and are part of, one physical body. We all breathe the same air, drink the same water, walk on the same Earth. We enter the world through the body of another being, share the same genes and DNA with others; share

21

the same molecules and atoms which when we die are released back into the biosphere again to be recycled into other beings. There is not a single being that could exist alone or in isolation. It defies creation. It defies science. We are interdependent and connected out of necessity. No being can do all things. We need others to fill the gaps. This is the way the Universe creates.

So why do we feel alone? I can only think at the moment that it is because we do not know who we are. We stunt ourselves with our classifications of gender, race and class, differences that are mostly superficial and which ignore this common nearly 14 billion year energy that is burning in all of us. We fetter ourselves when we create divisions of land, boundaries that are only human made – as if this four billion year old world and all that it took to create it, could possibly be 'owned' or possessed by a newly arrived and entirely dependent species. I wonder what that tells us about our sense of self that we imagine we can buy and sell the very entity that brought us forth?

We delude ourselves when we act from the belief that superiority of being, of intelligence, of ethic, lies in the colour of the outward layer of skin that covers our body and fool ourselves even further when we think that only institutions and scripture can hold the key to the divine. We insult ourselves when we ignore the fact that the human being first emerged in Africa and at our peril we ignore our debt to that continent and to those brave explorers who ventured into the unknown some hundred thousand years ago and began to cross the globe, seeking new frontiers, new experiences, new ways of living.

We diminish all that we are and hinder all that we might be, when we refuse to see our humanity in the entirety of its history. We could not have evolved without all that happened before us. We carry evolution in our body. We are part of this Universe. Life has brought us forth. Life is sustaining us. Our relatedness is basic to our existence, it is that which gives us life. The origin of all things from one source. How could it be any other way?

Earth is Primary, human is derivative.

Although this statement may be self–evident, if we honestly believed it to be true we would possibly have a very different relationship with Earth, one that was more respectful. Our Earth was created first. Not only that but it took a further four billion years of evolution before the conditions were favourable for a human being. In this time, the atmosphere changed, the dinosaurs had become extinct (but not before they had roamed for 250 million years) and so mammals could evolve in this niche evolution had created. They did this within the possibilities and limitations of the planet. Earth and its processes enabling such a creature to come into being, Earth and its processes setting the boundaries on what this creature could be. Earth, as primary, as first, the place that birthed life and amidst it, maybe as an accident, definitely as an afterthought, humanity. We are utterly dependent here. No Earth, no human. Scientists Carl Sagan and Neil deGrasse Tyson use the concept of the cosmic calendar to emphasize this point. They teach how if the Universe timescale was condensed to fit into one calendar year with the Big Bang occurring on the 1st of January, then we, the human, only arrive a few minutes before midnight on the 31st of December, the last day of that year. That is how new we are. We are derived from the possibilities that preceded us.

Differentiation, Communion and Interiority

The first principle I will talk about is how everything that exists in this Universe is characterised by Differentiation, Interiority and Communion. If either of these three dimensions of the Universe were removed, the Universe itself would collapse. The core of this principle is echoed in Berry's beautiful phrase that we are a communion of subjects and not a collection of objects. In its essence, this principle states that everything is different, everything exists in communion and everything has an interior or an inside life. Those are the facts told in a simple manner. The consequences and implications of this are much greater. But first let me say a bit more about this principle.

Differentiation

Differentiation refers to the fact that there are no two things the same since the beginning of time. Absolutely nothing. No two days, no two trees, no two people. No creature has ever lived who is the same as one who went before. Like all in the Universe we are a one-time creation, irreversible and non-repeatable, dependent on all and yet distinct. Not only that but it took all the past events of the Universe, all its processes of 13.8 billion years of development and creation for me and every Other living now, to be brought into being. The seamlessness of life connecting millennia. And yet difference scares us and to let people be who they are and not who we wish them to be is difficult for us. But we live in a Universe that exalts in diversity. We only need to look around us to witness this diversity- the oak, the ash, the thistle, the butterfly, the bee, the bird. We could spend a lifetime identifying creatures, each creature of a species with their own personality, their own individuality, their very own perspective on life.

On our birth we are supplied with a "*single finite quantum of energy and with this we are to identify who we are*"1. With this quantum of energy that we mould to become uniquely 'I' we give expression to who we are by engaging in the most fundamental act of the Universe which is creativity. Creativity, not solely in the sense of an artist creating her art but creativity in how each day we engage in the world, in how we create our friendships, our conversations, our lives and our experiences, of how we share these experiences. And each person does this differently. Conformity can be an easier option than risking the exploration of who you might be but we are not born to be the same, we are born to be who we uniquely are, and in this Universe, that is to be different.

Communion

Communion refers to the fact that we are all connected. Firstly, we all share the same source, a common origin. Not only this, but we all share the same atoms and molecules and are put together with the same particles. American astro-physicist Neil deGrasse Tyson writes:

> *...the very molecules that make up your body, the atoms that construct the molecules, are traceable to the crucibles that were once the centers of high mass stars that exploded their chemically rich guts into the galaxy, enriching pristine gas clouds with the chemistry of life so that we are all connected to each other biologically, to the Earth chemically and to the rest of the Universe atomically.*[2]

So interwoven are we into the fabric of this Universe, so deep our belonging, that the water in our bodies contains primordial hydrogen that was formed after the Big Bang; the iron in our blood was formed in the belly of a star that has since died and released its elements making the formation of Earth a possibility. We are in the Universe but equally and as significantly, the Universe is in us. It does not exist 'out there' somewhere beyond the Milky Way, it is in us. It is not the background to our existence but the very context from which we arise into being. Our bipedal bodies were shaped by our environment, by our need to eat and be secure; our rotating shoulders shaped by our arboreal ancestors, our freed arms and opposing thumbs so we could manipulate objects. The world has sculpted us, not only our body but also our consciousness and our spirituality. We need the scent of roses and the height of mountains to grow our thoughts. We need the whistling wind and crashing oceans to stir our spirit. We need to hear the lark at dawn and to see the horse in gallop to know who we are, to know that we are part of this world, coming from natural process and not separate to them. We exist only with others, only in communion.

If we are part of this world and if the Universe exists in us then we are instances and examples of how the world works and not an exception to it. We are not an addendum nor an appendage, not dropped into the world from space but we are an integral and wholly natural part of this Earth and this Universe.

Interiority

When we close our eyes and block the world out, we can become aware of our own Interiority, the inside of us. Another name for this is our subjectivity, that part that differentiates us as unique. Interiority refers to the inner life of every living being be they plant, cell, tree or human. As humans our spirit is most accessible through our interiority; an interiority that is present in all living 'beings' including Earth. This is our own self, our 'I', the deepest place/part of our being where we hold all that we are, our memories, hopes, desires, thoughts, feelings, happenings. This is the part of us that experiences. It is the essence of us. It is in Berry's words our 'numinous aspect.' Jesuit priest and palaeontologist, Pierre Teilhard de Chardin named this 'the spirit of matter.' According to Teilhard, in addition to its apparent physicality, all matter has a psychic component, a 'within', its own subjectivity and perspective. This subjectivity he called Radial Energy and in its simplest explanation refers to the tendency at every level, physically and mentally to self-organise. It is deeper than self-expression because it is greater than the self being expressed. It requires a creative response to the physical and psychic dimensions of our reality. The difficulty, and what has been forgotten in these times of mass-production and generic inculturation, is that there is no template or model for us to follow. As mentioned above, no person or creature has ever lived who is the same as one who went before. In particular in humanity, there is no blueprint for how we are to become fully ourselves or express this interiority. This is for us to discover.

The world is always coming to us whether it is tangible or directly observable to us or not. It comes to us through our dreams, our emotions, our intuitions. Poet and philosopher Maria Rainer Rilke wrote *'words are the last resort for what lies deep within'* and often we feel the mystery, the awe, the stirring of some eternal awareness before we can articulate it. It is beyond our conscious thought, beyond our rational mind but we feel it catch in our throat when we are struck by moments of sadness, we feel it expand in our belly at moments of great beauty, quiet our thoughts in moments of tenderness. The way in which we express this awareness is the unique creative act of each person. Our interiority articulated in diversity which can only be witnessed in communion.

These Principles at Work in the Universe

We can see these principles present in both the macro-cosmos and the micro-cosmos. Again, think of a flower. The stalk differs from the petals and the petals differ from the carpel but together these parts make up what it is to be a flower. Communion in diversity. We can also see the flower's interiority at work in that she somehow, with the endowment of water and sun can organise herself to emerge from her seed, deposit her roots and gradually grow her constituent parts until the time arrives where she is ready to fully announce herself to the world and she opens her petals one by one and blooms. Her communion drawing forth her diversity, for it is not the stalk that makes the flower bloom but the entire flower together, her diversity enhancing her communion in that mysterious way the Universe has of making the whole greater than the sum of parts, and her interiority ensuring that she can bring about this wondrous act.

Then above that beautiful flower, we can see these laws at work in Earth herself. The flower being part of Earth and the one who describes the flower being part of Earth. Each being emphasizing the unique qualities of the other; each being unable to do what the other does but equally unable to be who they are without the presence of the other. The flower fertilising, the human admiring and describing. Both of them part of the larger event that is called Earth. Their very relatedness and difference making Earth the wondrous place it is. We can also see Earth's interiority reflected in its ability to adapt, take the example we used earlier of how although the sun has increased in temperature by 25% in the past four billion years, Earth has maintained its surface temperature allowing life to flourish.

And far even beyond the sun and past the space between our solar system and other stars, this law is also at work in the Milky Way galaxy. It spins together, as a unit, in communion but inside it there are over 300 billion stars including our own sun and possibly eight billion planets including the eight planets making up our solar system. There is us, seven billion people oblivious to the fact that we are rotating through space. Even within our own limited terms of reference we can see from our neighbouring planets the diversity that is in the Milky Way. And how in some way, all this differentiation acts together and moves as one. The moon controlling our tides and gravity, the sun feeding us, Mars piquing our curiosity and wonder. But more than this, we witness again the power of interiority and the subjectivity of this galaxy in how it has organised itself, in how it disperses its contents and enables individual self-organising elements to arise within it, in how it spins steadily through space as a unit, revolving around the other galaxies and constellations, in how it creates itself amidst all the immensity.

These Principles at Work in Me

We are part of this Universe. It is in us. The laws that govern it also govern us and yet, as a species, we act as if we are separate. For many, we have yet to realise that our actions have consequences and for every action there is a reaction. For others, the Earth has been desacralized, its intrinsic value and holiness, even its beauty, lost on a people who see life as beginning and ending with their own birth and death.

But what would the world be like if we worked from this principle, that each and every being has an inner life that contains the sacred, that contains that same divine energy which has been travelling since the beginning of time? That not only my own thoughts and my own feelings and my own wounds and aspirations are precious but so too are those of every person I meet, every eye I look into, every creature I dismiss or criticise or condemn? Or kill. No being exists outside of the sacred and divine energy that is this Universe. The Divine, in whatever you imagine divinity to be, radiates from each one of us. Life may have dampened us and coloured our view and thwarted our desires, but that sacredness is still housed within us moving through all our tribulations, all our moods, waiting for us to let it be expressed and to bring it forth. This is the very same sacredness that lies in others waiting to be recognised and respected and acknowledged in them, just as we acknowledge it in ourselves.

Or if we lived from the law that each being is meant to be different, that in fact we are brought forth to give fresh expression to the world? Then, difference would become a value. In a simplistic way, we wouldn't be competing to be the best at the same thing, we would be cooperating to help each other bring forth what we are each best at. That the most authentic life, the most fulfilling life is to be who we are insomuch as this way does not harm myself or others and to let others be fully who they are so that we are always openhearted and receptive welcoming the Divine in all the ways she has manifest. Is this not in direct contrast to those who seek homogeny, who practise racism and sexism, homophobia or any ideology that claims the truth as their own? Could we imagine a world that was all the same, entirely, without difference? The monotony of nothing new to be discovered or learned because we would know everything already, of nothing to amaze us or awe us because it is exactly as we are, of nothing or no-one to surprise us and lift us from our preconception with the gentle joy of feeling foolish. Can you imagine the hell that is the endless drudgery of sameness where nothing new can grow until we suffocate in our own repetition and staleness of spirit?

Or if we lived from the principle, that we are not the only ones who matter; that our lives are deeply connected with everyone else's and all of our actions will have a result, that we can only be here because of others. We are connected to the stars, to the protons from the sun and the green plants that convert it into energy, to the Earth worm that fertilises the soil, the bee who pollinates the flowers and the bacteria that helps us to digest our food. It is a world of connectedness, of relationship.

Wouldn't this make us think twice about our words and our deeds, about how we choose to expend the energy that is me, in how we choose to pass it on? Wouldn't this make us think twice about how we want to live our brief and precious time here on Earth and what we would like to contribute during our time here?

Cosmogenesis and Complexity-Consciousness
- Pierre Teilhard de Chardin

The next principle or law I would like to speak about is Cosmogenesis but before I do, it is important to speak about Pierre Teilhard de Chardin. Teilhard was a French palaeontologist and a Jesuit priest. He was one of the first to realise and transmit the view that the Universe story and the human story are inseparable. He described how the evolutionary Universe had brought forth the human. His spirituality was one that was immersed in the physical realities of the world. Matter for him was sacred and revealed God. For this, he was criticised by theologians and scientists alike. And yet this way of seeing the world and of relating to God was not new. Earlier, American philosopher and writer, Ralph Waldo Emerson who died the year after Teilhard was born had written "*there seems to be a necessity in spirit to manifest itself in material forms…….. the visible creation is the terminus or circumference of the invisible world* "[3]. Today, both the ideas of Teilhard and Emerson are crying out to be heard, their relevancy all the more urgent for the rapid transformation the human must undergo in how it views its place and role in the world and in how it views the world itself. Poignantly, Teilhard wrote "*one could*

say that the whole of life lies in seeing....to try and see more and
to see better is not, therefore, just a fantasy, curiosity, or a luxury.
See or perish"4. How we see the world and how we see each other
has consequences, what we learn about and spend our thoughts on
has consequences. Our view of reality will determine the way in
which we participate in the world, this is why the vision and
knowledge Teilhard has brought to the world is so important. This
section will focus on two of his most important insights
'Cosmogenesis' and 'Complexity- consciousness'.

Cosmogenesis

One of the most significant insights from science about
our Universe, in my view, is that it is not a fixed, unchanging
object. It is constantly giving birth to itself and creating itself
anew. This is what the Universe does. It creates. It is a work in
progress, a world that is, but that is also becoming, a Universe that
is developing through time. Teilhard called this Cosmogenesis. To
say this implies that our Universe is unfinished which in turn
might imply that it has an endpoint or a destination. This is
something that leading proponents of this story have surmised
about. Brian Swimme, mathematical cosmologist, who co-
authored The Universe Story with Thomas Berry has written how
the Universe may be 'building something' while Teilhard believed
the Universe was 'going somewhere'. This is the idea that over
time the Universe is becoming more, increasing its ability for
experience, for beauty, for feeling. If it is gradually becoming
more, if the Divine (as suggested by Jean Gebser) is gradually
becoming more manifest, being revealed in our capacity to love, to
feel compassion, in the Earth's capacity to direct a flock of starling
in an Israeli sky, then perhaps it will not stop until that which lies
at the foundation of this world is expressed in its entirety. But
what evidence is there of this possibility?

Since its beginnings, the Universe has developed and
changed, always becoming more than it was, always transcending
itself. The release of energy with the Big Bang creating hydrogen

and helium, which in time transformed into stars and galaxies. The death of a star enabling the birth of a solar system. Teilhard de Chardin writes *"the evolution of matter {is} in current theory, the gradual building up, by increasing complication, of the various elements recognised by physiochemistry"*[5]. Duncan and Tyler in Our Cosmic Context write *"the existence of life as we know it is really a property of the whole Universe, not just an isolated feature of the planet Earth. For starters, the elements needed as the building blocks for life were formed long ago in other stars and in the Big Bang."* [6]

Palaeontologist, Richard Fortey also makes a nod towards this point when he writes *"the placement of the Earth in the firmament, and its pivoting in the solar system, are fine-tuned to make life a possibility. If life is just a matter of chance, then the dice were loaded in its favour"*[7]. The Universe builds on what went before it but with each transformation becomes more than it was. My favourite description of this, although not scientific, is American poet Drew Dillinger's line from his poem 'Hymn to the Sacred Body of the Universe' where he writes *'the poet says 'this entire travelling Cosmos is the secret One, slowly growing a body'*[8]. The secret One slowly growing a body, spirit that is gradually becoming flesh, opaque becoming transparent.

Let us park this speculation for a moment and let us think about change which as we can see is a fundamental behaviour of this Universe. It can be difficult to imagine that there was a time when there was no Earth, when it had not yet been written into existence. Equally difficult to comprehend that the Universe was over nine billion years old, over two thirds of its current age when Earth was formed, making Earth a recent event. We look at our planet today pulsing with life, so vibrant in colour and beauty, smell and sound and again find it difficult to imagine that Earth was not always as she is now but was once a fiery, molten rock.

So many times we hear the phrase that 'there is nothing new under the sun'. But everything under the sun is new. Here now on Earth, some four billion years later, every moment is new, bringing with it something that had not existed previously whether it be a new ray of sun recently created and arriving on our planet with its light and warmth, a new life, or a new thought gained from a new experience, or a new experience itself, all fresh expressions of a Universe that cannot create the same thing twice.

There will also come a time when Earth in turn will cease to exist. Earth is not exempt from the flow of birth, death and rebirth that keeps this Universe creative and moving, nor am I. The Universe is not a place it is a journey. A journey that is unfolding, a journey marked by what emerges and what is born and how these 'events' shape what will come next. There is not a fixed space or time or event that is pre-set for us that we will walk into. Rather as philosopher Alfred North Whitehead wrote, we arise out of our previous experiences which are shaped by our environment and those we interact with and through our actions, choices and decisions, we create our future. And this is cosmogenesis, our ability and our responsibility to create something that is new, within an entity that is itself, endlessly creative.

Complexity-Consciousness

Connected to the above point is Teilhard's idea of complexity consciousness. The more complex an organism is in its make-up, the more intense forms of interiority that are associated with it. As life has evolved it has become progressively more complex beginning with the single cell organism right up to the multi-cellular organisms, to eventually the animal and human organisms which are self-organising and self-governing. Although radial energy exists in all organisms, it is less developed in the earlier and more simply designed ones. Teilhard's point was that as life evolves it complexifies, using more intricate and interconnected parts, and with this complexification comes a corresponding increase in interiority and depth. Teilhard believed that this was evident in the human being, one of the last species to arrive on Earth and the only species that as of now we are able to ascertain, who has self-reflective consciousness – the creature who knows that she knows, the creature who can reflect on her existence and on herself. It is this self-reflective consciousness which has become a new medium for evolutionary processes, but more of this in the next chapter.

I stated earlier, how the Universe has the mystical quality of transcending itself, of continuously becoming more than it was so that the whole is always greater than the sum of its parts. Take the example again of the human being, a biological creature who emerged from biological processes yet containing some element be it spirit, psyche or consciousness which seems to transcend biology, to sit outside time and events and to relate to the world in a way that is not just physical or biological but that is transcendent of them. Or, the example of how dust and gas and particles congeal and mould to become a solar system which includes our very own diverse planet and all that have their being on it. And this is the mystery, that in some way using the elements it has, the Universe can become more than it was.

These are some of the principles or laws of our Universe, principles that great minds such as Thomas Berry, such as Brian Swimme and Jim Conlon, have realised and articulated. But what do these mean for my own short, human life?

Chapter 4
The Self-Reflective Creature

I spoke earlier of the externalities of our world but we also live an interior life as full as the physical life wherein is planted our being, whispering inside us constantly and interpreting the world for us. We call it thought, we call it reflection, we call it consciousness. To some it is the expression of the soul; to others it is an awareness of our being amidst the being of others. We say that it lives in the mind but we are not sure where the mind is. We say that it is the brain but have an intuition that it is more than the brain, that it is the body but that it is more than the body. We say that it is the combined working of all these together – the mind, the body, the brain and the spirit. We 'know' that it is the part of us that can objectify what 'I' am feeling and thinking, and organize and articulate it so that another 'I' can understand it. We know that it is the part of us that dreams and hopes and imagines, that analyses these dreams and hopes and encourages or dissuades them; that reads another's face to try and gauge their feeling and then assimilates a response to that feeling; that feels the sun warm on our face and knows that it is the sun that is warming our face.

Carl Jung once wrote that there are as many galaxies within a human being as there are without and perhaps one of the deepest mysteries of our species is this, our ability to reflect, so that as we walk around attending to the daily burdensome, humdrum and banal aspects of life, to the administration of living that our civilization has necessitated, we are simultaneously walking around as recipients and vehicles of that spark of consciousness that must have been birthed in the initial flaring forth some 14 billion years ago. This spark has now come to develop in the human in the form of an internal life as complex as our physical reality, which is both interdependent with, and helps to shape, this reality.

But what is self- reflective consciousness? What is this ability to be able to think about ourselves, to feel emotion and passion and desire and to be able to ask why? To think and question our thoughts? To examine ourselves and our world almost as if we were observers and not participants?

Consciousness

I have struggled to know what consciousness is, to be able to define it and to understand its importance as a human capacity. I have listened to people talk of creating a 'New Consciousness' as the way in which to begin healing our planet - raise people's awareness, make us think about our actions, a change in consciousness being the only way in which we change the way we relate to Earth. Is this what is needed - is the change entirely dependent on how we are conscious? Has our consciousness the power to mitigate and heal the ecological devastation that we are responsible for?

In struggling to understand this powerful phenomenon, I have read the many words of others in the hope that their studies might shed light on this strange ability. Although there are many different interpretations about what consciousness might be and how we have come to possess it, it still remains a nebulous concept inexplicable either by science or philosophy. There is some commonality of thought however in that it is generally agreed that consciousness is our instrument, or the name given to our faculty of understanding ourselves, the Earth and the Universe we are part of and as we pass through time or as time passes through us, it is gradually becoming more and more refined.

Consciousness in the Individual

From my own studies and experience I have come to learn that there are primarily two ways of knowing. One of these is knowing with the intellect. This means understanding an idea or concept, formulating and organising an idea or concept or holding information or memories. The other is knowing with the heart, i.e knowing something to be true and implicit in or applicable to oneself. Pascal writes '*the heart is reason that reason knows not of*'. I agree with him, I think that we also reason in our heart in a way that differs from the mind. The heart's reason is the reason of compassion and the reason of justice and equity, not always logical or deductible, not always explanatory but reason nonetheless in that it is a deep, primal knowing that hasn't yet found sufficient articulation or a category in the mind. It is the place where we hold the history of our truths. It is also the reason of love.

It is my view that when these two forms of knowledge combine they create 'Consciousness' which is an awareness that is deeper than intellect but uses intellect as one means of expression. Other means of expression might be art, poetry or dance. Alfred North Whitehead, the process-relational philosopher writes of occasions as "drops of experience" and that our individual drops of experience are held together and unified by our consciousness, that our consciousness is the flow of the body's experience or feeling. Consciousness in this sense is similar to the role of the soul or the personality and it is that which unites or integrates a person. I often think that all our other senses are at the service of our consciousness, in that they all 'work' in a way that is reflective of how we 'see' things. Our understanding of things is also related in some way to our consciousness. We are the creature named 'Homo sapiens sapiens' the one who knows they know, what it is we know is unclear but we are aware that it is 'I' who am looking at the tree and that the tree is in some way different to me. It is almost as if we intuit that there is *something* to know, and in seeking to know we give interpretation and build meaning from the Universe. These interpretations and meanings do not remain static but are adjusted or transformed as we accumulate more experience, which in turn affects and alters our consciousness.

Interestingly, Duncan in 'The Cosmic Context' writes that one of the distinctions between early hominids and modern humans is the ability to tell lies, which would suggest the beginning of the realisation that we as human beings are conscious beings. He writes *"the ability to deceive others is a significant one, because it means you understand how* they *see things"*[1]. So not only do we understand or are conscious in our own right but we can also gauge the understanding or consciousness of another. We can do this through what the person says and how they behave. The significance of this is that it increases understanding from subjective to objective, increases our awareness of ourselves into our awareness of others, as well as what we perceive *them* to be aware of, and brings with it the seeds of power and the seeds of compassion, but also perhaps the beginning of feelings of isolation and separation. We have used this mysterious, almost transcendental ability to the detriment of our species, creating a powerful weapon which masks and manipulates reality, creates illusions of knowledge and blurs the boundary of wants and needs. And although there is not one among us who cannot lie successfully, there are few among us who can know when they are being lied to. And yet we must have stumbled upon this remarkable power of deception, fallen upon its seductive power. It must have initially been a surprise and perhaps there was a long and laboured communication to clear away the misunderstanding but when did we put it in our pocket, this skill, when did we commit it to memory and hone it and refine it so that it could become an interior manipulation of externality, of dreams, of others?

Consciousness within a Society;
and Gebser's Structures of Consciousness

Consciousness within a society is more difficult to describe but it has a large effect on the capabilities and actions of humans often without our knowledge. Thomas Berry and Brian Swimme have written that human self-consciousness can be characterised by five phases, these being: the primordial emergence of the human; the Neolithic settlements; the classical civilizations; the rise of nations and the Ecozoic Era. There is little doubt that our consciousness, collectively, has changed through and with, time and history. To some degree we are aware of more now than we were previously – we know more about how the world works in a scientific sense, we know more about systems of oppression and domination, we are coming to know more about the insidious power of marketing and corporations; we know more about our history and this has enabled us to see things and events differently and has led to civil rights movements to change behaviour and action, such as the abolition of slavery, black rights, women's rights and gay rights. It is difficult to say whether the change in consciousness came first or whether the experience came first. Either way there seems to be a correlation between the two. What we know has expanded but there is also evidence that it has diminished, particularly in the last centuries, in relation to our place in the cosmos and our relationship with other creatures.

In 1949, German-born philosopher and linguist Jean Gebser wrote about the different structures and stages of consciousness in his book 'The Ever-Present Origin'. He says that human consciousness structures go through a mutation and that the development of different structures of consciousness is not always linear. Although he describes four different phases or structures of consciousness historically, he states that all phases can be found in any particular structure. Gebser names the four stages of consciousness as:

1) The Archaic
2) The Magical
3) The Mythical
4) The Mental.

Each stage reaches its peak when its contribution to consciousness is most complete and then it begins to become "deficient". According to Gebser, we are currently living through the deficient mode of the mental where rationality and logic has contributed all it can to our consciousness and has now become an obstacle to our learning.

In the archaic structure humanity does not differentiate between himself/herself and her surrounding environments. During this period '*the experience of the human being, that is consciousness, was totally identical with the whole*'2 and consciousness is undifferentiated. In the magical structure people lived in a group or tribal consciousness and '*any event is unitary, is a space-time event, and that any event, entity, activity can be exchanged for any other. In this sense the soul is not yet inside but strewn among all events*'3. This structure differs from the archaic in that during archaic consciousness there is a single identity between consciousness and the world, whilst in the magical there is unity, and humanity has not yet distinguished itself from nature. In the mythical structure when humanity became aware of the psyche or interiority, time is characterised as circular and there is also a polarity in division e.g. male and female, Earth and sky. It was in this structure that language first began to be developed and where the dominant mode of experience is feeling. Lastly, the mental structure is defined by the rise of rational thought and where the human fully develops his separation from nature and the ego or individual self is born. Each structure becomes deficient when that which illuminated it is no longer effectual. According to Gebser, we are currently living through the deficient mode of the mental and are now constrained by rationality and logic. During the Paleolithic era or what Jean Gebser calls the magical age, consciousness of fire, of the cycles of life and death produced rituals and arts. During the early civilizations or Gebser's mythical age, consciousness of feelings and the finiteness of the human condition produced a relationship with the Gods. During the Industrial or the mental age, consciousness of resources and how to utilize them produced machines and technology and the idea of progress. During all these times consciousness produced the defining narratives of the day. Consciousness was people's means of taking in the world around them and then relating to that world, it was the building block from which they constructed their world view.

I am not sure how consciousness can become collective in a society. In fact societies have different forms of consciousness simultaneously. How then does one consciousness become more dominant and how does one form of consciousness become the norm? Is the collective consciousness of a society affected by the power and wealth of individuals or can a collective consciousness encapsulate and transcend its individuals e.g. like the mob mentality taking on a life of its own so that it cannot be affected or influenced? And if consciousness contains some element of divine understanding how is it present in consciousness' like this?

Thinking about consciousness raises more questions than it answers. If consciousness only occurs along with a knowing of the heart it can only be changed with an individual realisation. This raises two questions – how can there ever be an illuminated collective consciousness and how can somebody change somebody else's consciousness when it is significantly dependent on internal factors such as heart knowledge and the divine? Such questions only serve to deepen the mystery of what consciousness is and to highlight the futility and frustration in thinking about the world in terms of collective or personal. Does one not presuppose another? If I am part of the group do I not bring my own consciousness to bear on that group thus adjusting and affecting the overall consciousness? And yet one cannot deny the growing mind that is accumulating and how this mind is empowering humanity to achieve things that would have been unimaginable, one also cannot deny that at the base of this mind and this consciousness, driving it to further and further exploration, is curiosity.

The Power of Consciousness

Whether we call it thought, reflection or consciousness there is no denying what this capacity has illuminated for

41

humanity. Perhaps another word is to say 'discovered' but are we not just beginning to see what has always been there, each new discovery adding to our understanding of this Universe and ourselves, as if the Universe is unfolding herself to us, slowly unveiling the majesty, precision and elegance of her workings?

Todd Duncan in his book 'Your Cosmic Context' writes how human intelligence, in order for it to have evolved in the way that it has, must have had some social benefit. Duncan calls it intelligence but what is intelligence only the interpretation and synthesis of knowledge gathered and what is consciousness only our awareness of knowledge? We do not have to think hard to see what some of these benefits to our species have been. Think of a life without language, although not the only means of communication, it has provided a depth of articulation of the interior giving us insight in to and expression of such things as emotions and desires, giving us insight into our own nature. David Abram in his book "The Spell of the Sensuous" puts forward a theory of language. He writes that being creatures who were deeply immersed in nature we took in the sounds of our environment. We listened to the bellowing of animals, the whispering of the trees, the crashing of waves, to the birds singing. These sounds coalesced some place deep within the human, deep in our interior being and then eventually came back out as human language initially expressed in groans and grunts until eventually expressed in word and symbol that were recognizable to others.

From language, we developed characters and letters, an alphabet of symbols marked in matter, enabling information to be written down, preserved and passed on, contributing to the accumulation of this mind that we are building. And how did somebody, one day, stumble across vegetable oil as a means of making ink and developed and developed it until it became the pen that can be brought everywhere, allowing this magical, alchemous act of turning thought into word and word into matter occur at any time and in any place; of freezing time and events, people and places so that we can recall it over and over again and evoke the experience in others who were not a witness?

We made instruments from the trees and imitating the birds, we filled the air with song for the sheer pleasure of listening to melody. We created games and sport so that all the community could become involved and using our bodies as instruments we evoked in people the emotions of excitement and anticipation, of pride and good-will, for absolute enjoyment and as homage to the form that we walk through life in. We created dance. All of these are a response to the Universe, an expression of her sounds and colours and textures, stirring the human consciousness, awakening its curiosity and wonder and compelling us to create.

We built boats that enabled us to sail across the oceans, indulging the curiosity that lingers at the foundation of our being and at the foundation of our consciousness. At first, boats made of logs and bamboo, then boats with sails whipped by the wind, then ships made of metal which can carry cars and planes and canons and weapons. We learned how to control disease such as Smallpox and Tuberculosis increasing the lives and decreasing the suffering of many people. We built pyramids and cathedrals and mosques reaching to the sky and praising the Gods until we eventually took to the skies ourselves, building aeroplanes and jets heavier than air which hold hundreds of people and can travel thousands of miles. It's always astounding for me to see a tin-box hurtling through the clouds thousands of feet above me holding all these people. In my head I imagine them to be small, Lego-like people, smiling and happy and bendable in the centre. But they're not, they're real and living, I'm one of them, and they are stepping in to this machine that will fly them across the continents and they will step out into foreign lands and explore the diversity of cultures and foods and language there as if it is the most natural thing in the world. And maybe it is.

We interpret the magnetic waves from the sun and build radios transmitting information and song and connecting people all over the world. We later harness these waves and use them to build machines to fight cancerous cells in our bodies. We tentatively begin to probe space, we map and name the stellar constellations and learn how they were formed. A human being stands upon the moon and a shuttle is launched that will take pictures of our galaxy and Earth like we have never seen before, bringing images of the stars light years away into our sitting rooms, into our minds and into our heart. The curiosity that comes from our consciousness with the know-how that comes from our consciousness taking pictures of the Earth whereon we stand which begins to change our consciousness.

The power of this phenomenon is undeniable, as with each new insight, each new discovery our lives our altered. It is a mysterious force, living in the individual and beyond the individual, living in the collective but also beyond the collective, shaping us and shaping our world sometimes explicitly and other times implicitly. It travels invisibly but we recognize its presence by the visible results of its effect; perhaps it travels on the light waves of this Universe, perhaps carried by the wind, or maybe it does not travel at all but like love is always there and is brought to life through desire, through curiosity and the 'need to know', the human being always seeking more and more and more, as if we are somehow unfinished and incomplete, drawing the evolution forward, wanting to be whole.

Consciousness in Being

There is an old Buddhist saying which even though I cannot remember when it was said or who said it, that I have never forgotten. It is in regards to speech and how I remember it is that we should only say something if it meets the following three criteria – Is it true? Is it necessary? Is it kind? If it does not meet these criteria then it should never be spoken. Our words reflect our consciousness; the words of others shape our consciousness. It is a world that is saturated with words, opinions, thoughts, theories, theses', books, plays, essays and poems. A world that is saturated with consciousness and the expression of consciousness.

44

But we are also physical beings. We walk on the Earth with our feet that were formed by it. We breathe the air through our nose and bending our legs lean down and smell the lily. We swim in the ocean and climb the mountains. On a sunny day, we lie on the short, wiry grass amongst the primroses and listen to the creek as it meanders and gurgles through the riverbed, carving its own path, small but no less determined than the larger river that spawned it. We squish our toes into the sand, the welcome mat of the ocean, and squeal as they sink into the watery, softness of it, grainy and small and golden. We stand in the sea, its icy coldness lapping us, exhilarating our bodies with its curious pleasure, making us breathe deeper and sharper, the effect of one element upon another. We walk through the thick green forests, breathing in the pine, so fresh, so living, and listen as the autumn leaves crackle under our feet. We watch the hummingbird as it hovers skilfully, beating its wings faster than sight, and wonder can it feel our presence, our admiration for its dexterity and grace? We pick the bright blooming flowers and take them inside so that our own nest may become beautiful and scented. We are the human element as bound into the web of life as any other creature. We are not *the* web of life but we make it sweeter because we can live it and know we are living it, because we can smell it and know its scent. We are as natural and as physical a creature or process that has ever lived, differentiated by our consciousness. It is my view that our consciousness comes *with* our physical being, not before it, or after it, or above it.

With this consciousness, comes great responsibility. Whether there are greater or lesser degrees of consciousness is not the point to focus on; whether there are enlightened consciousness' or a consciousness that remains ignorant is also not the point to focus on. No consciousness develops separate to our physical reality. They are hand in hand, related, dependent and intertwined. They each are because of the other, the same energy manifest differently. We cannot privilege our consciousness above our planet nor can we go through life as if we are solely matter and refuse to engage with our mind- refuse to ask the questions of why we are here, how should we be living, do we matter, where are we going? It is one entity and the diminishment of either affects the other. We need our consciousness to appreciate and protect our planet and we need our planet to stir and activate our consciousness.

This brings me back to the Buddhist saying I mentioned earlier, it also brings to mind the Second Law of Thermodynamics which relates to the fact that all the energy of the Universe is needed by the entire Universe and that no new energy is being created. Everything we do, every thought we think uses energy. If we spend our energy on one thing then by the law of the Universe we will have less energy to spend on something else. How important and limited our energy is and yet we seem to be so careless in our use of it. Would I choose my actions and my thoughts more carefully if I were aware of the finiteness of my energy? Would I choose my words more kindly if I thought they were going towards the sustenance of this energy? This is true of our body, as we get older we are more considering in what we do physically. It should also be true of our 'consciousness' whether that is our intelligence, our emotions or our spirit, whatever we may call this gift, its presence can only be lived through the body whether by word or action, its effect can only be seen in our treatment of others and in the treatment of our Earth and all the creatures that have their home here.

Does a change in consciousness happen before the experience or does the experience create a change in consciousness? I do not know how we learn to think and feel and interpret differently. Nor do I know definitively when it is time for us to start to think differently or 'to change our consciousness'. I do know that it has been the consciousness of the industrial and post-industrial era that has been responsible for the belief that the human being is separate to nature; an addendum and not a process of the Earth's functioning; a mechanistic, dualistic and individual consciousness that is responsible for the destruction and devastation our planet is living through now.

We are thinking, reflective Earth; part of this singular event that is the Universe, curious and desiring in nature, exploring the depths of ourselves and all that has brought us forth. We have become aware of so much as a species and now we need to stop, to lay down our pens and cameras and machines, take our fingers off the keyboard, silence the cellphone and think about what we have learnt, think about the knowledge that we have gathered and what it means, what it shows us, until it seeps into our mind and into our heart, until it becomes our wisdom and we begin to walk upon the Earth as contributors to the whole, assemblers of the jigsaw, and lovers of the creation. Ask the big questions!

Chapter 5
Poverty and Abundance

Last summer was one of the hottest this country has had in years. The days were hazy and blue and the sun brought a balmy tranquillity that slowed people down. It was on one of these days that I sat on the footpath on a laneway off Grafton St. I was eating an orange whose taste was full and sweet and whose colour was all the brighter under the radiant light of the sun. As its juice trickled down my chin in a delicious mess, I began to think of all that it had taken for that orange to ripen, and how this moment of enjoying that fruit first began to take place deep in the core of the sun some ninety-three million miles away from us.

First the sun, in its centre, has to burn hydrogen into helium which then spreads as radiation and travels through space until it reaches our planet as light and warmth. It takes approximately eight minutes for the sun's rays to reach Earth. This light and warmth, combined with the rains, falls on the seed of the orange tree until it is strong enough to put down its roots and anchor itself in the soil. The tree becomes stronger and begins to produce leaves and to flower which enable it to further capture the energy in the rays of the sun. The tree takes between 27-30 years to reach maturity but will start to produce edible fruit after only seven years. The orange is a result of this combined activity that starts in the sun and is continued on Earth, an inter-related and dependent series of events.

The process of nuclear reaction and combustion has been repeating itself over and over again in the centre of our sun for more than five billion years. It is the catalyst of Earth's own productivity. I thought about all that the sun in relationship with Earth produces. Everything we eat. Everything we drink. All the materials we use to build our homes and to clothe ourselves. It is so abundant and prolific in its produce, so generous. Hafiz said '*even after all this time, the sun never says to the Earth, 'you owe me'. Look what happens with a love like that, it lights up the whole sky.*' It lights up the whole sky and feeds an entire world. Or so it should do.

In 2008, the World Bank published statistics of how the world's consumption is distributed. It reported that the world's richest 20% consumed 76.6% of the world's total resources, while the world's poorest 20% consumed just 1.5% and the middle 60% consumed 21.9%. The same report noted how in a population that is currently 7 billion and growing, at least 80% of people live on less than $10 a day and over three billion (half the world's population) live on less than $2.50 a day. The universal standard of poverty (however misleading and uninformative) is less than one dollar a day. Nearly 22,000 children die every day of hunger or disease, and there are over 1 billion people who cannot read or write. It also highlighted how the gap between rich and poor is progressively widening, and how the money spent on arms and cosmetics far outweighs that spent on debt relief or development aid. The stark inequality and injustice of this begs the question of where it all went wrong. It is a mark of our dysfunction, of our disconnect with our surroundings and what we think we need that we live in a world that is abundant, and still people starve.

Consumption

It can be argued that we, particularly those of us in the global North, live in a consumerist society. We live in a way that our entire lives are oriented towards accumulation. We are, most of us, educated within the industrial-economic system and educated towards jobs and careers which will produce for this system. We go to university and colleges and earn degrees so that we can (to use Brian Swimme's wonderful phrase) accumulate more money to buy more things. Our garments, where we buy our food, where we go on holidays, the furniture we have inside our house, the cars that we drive, are all symbols of wealth. The more you have, the better you can buy. This has infiltrated every aspect of our lives so that there is nothing free from the power of marketing, down to as basic an item as a baby's nappy, up to and including a house. Our lives have somehow become defined by our consumption rate and our ability (financial or otherwise) to consume the best.

It is only people who have a certain level of income that can afford to spend like this and these people live mostly in the Northern hemisphere. I say mostly because it is not the rule. There are individuals of great wealth in every country but as the World Bank report shows and as the United Nations Development Programme also reports, 20%, only one fifth of the world's population, account for three quarters of the world's consumption. According to Wolfgang Sachs, environmentalist and scholar '*It is those 20% who eat 45% of all the meat and fish, consume 68% of all electricity, 84% of all the paper, and own 87% of all the automobiles*' 1. It is startlingly unequal. On my first reading of these statistics I thought how utterly, utterly unfair. Surely everyone is entitled to their share? But now I am not so sure what poverty is, if more is really more at all, whether we actually have any entitlements, and feel increasingly that in our desire to progress that we are headed the wrong way.

Poverty

From the years 2001-2004, I lived and worked on the Philippine Island of Mindanao. It is a beautiful island, lush and fertile and rich in fruits and fish and flowers. Near to the equator, the sun pours down on its rice terraces and seas and makes the sky there seem more blue, the greens more green and the reds more red. But it is also an economically poor island and classified as 'developing'. During the time I spent there I began to wonder about what it means to be poor and in our aspirations to 'develop' what were we aiming towards.

While there I observed that it was generally the case that people's basic needs were met. There was food. For those who were poorer it was not a varied diet, but generally corn based at all three meals with some vegetables and perhaps, during fiestas or special occasions, meat. There was water, often polluted but water nonetheless and there was tuba, a coconut wine which was also drunk. There was shelter, although insecure and extremely basic homes built of corrugated steel and wood. For the vast majority of people with whom I came into contact, there was no material surplus, no extra outfits of clothes or pairs of shoes, no pantries of food. But there seemed to me there was a freedom from having so little where life could be more about relationship than preoccupation about objects. There was a freedom (perhaps because there was very little choice otherwise - would people choose to have more if there was more available to them?) to appreciate the other aspects of life, chatting aimlessly in a payag by the sea; playing guitar and singing; resting after a meal. Life seemed unhurried to me where people lived in immediate presence with each other, where they had time to let each other respond and to just sit and pay attention to life as it unfolded around them.

After my time in Mindanao, I returned to Ireland. The Celtic tiger was in full swing and there was a prosperity about the country, an attitude of confidence and self-assurance which seems to come with the accumulation of wealth – a strange thing for money to be able to buy. I had not been home in three years and numerous new housing estates had sprung up around the town. People were dressed differently, they drove newer cars, were going on shopping holidays to New York. They were also working harder and longer hours. The lifestyle here was in contrast to the country that I had just left. People had more disposable income and so were able to buy more, but there was another consequence to this new found wealth. There seemed to be a growing sense of despair among people as life took on a frenetic pace and time was taken out of people's hands. Too much too quick. Since 1998 there have been an average of 500 deaths by suicide per year which puts Ireland's suicide rate at the fifth highest in the EU. Obviously, our new found wealth did not equate with contentment. In fact, to me there seemed to be a loss, a loss of time being our own and all that this incorporates, less time for each other, for chatting, for discovering and observing life, for simply paying attention to it. A loss of simplicity, a life that was more cluttered by objects, money and the pursuit of money. An emptiness from living concerned only with life's externalities. I thought about when I would die and the questions I would ask myself – how did I spend my life? Who did I spend it with? What did I contribute? Money seemed such a strange occupation.

I had grown up in an age where we were taught to feel sorry for those who were less well-off and who could not afford what we had. I went to work in the Philippines with this sentiment firmly ingrained in me, perhaps it was the reason I went in the first place. But the three years spent there, erased the pity from me and I began to experience life in a new and fresh way so that by the time I returned home, the way that people were living now made no sense to me and I became wistful for the country I had left, envious of how they lived – whether forced or not. I do not want to romanticise indigenous peoples or to glamorise material deprivation which brings its own suffering, but the fundamental attitude to life and to the world just seemed so much larger and full and generous than what I was witnessing now. I could not understand why we would give all our time and energy, even our principles, to making money and buying bigger and bigger houses, bigger and bigger cars. What did we think life was for? Why were we all rushing, what could we possibly do with all we owned? Why were we all so competitive? Where were the dreamers and the poets, the artists? Where was the depth and soulfulness of a people who had always had a heightened sense of life's mysteries? How had such an industrial, mechanistic, thought and spirit-numbing way of life seeped into our country? I know there was reasons we did it, consume so much, reasons that seemed rational and that can still seem rational when spoken by certain people today, but right then as it faced me, it seemed nothing short of madness.

Waste and Degradation

There are other consequences to this wealth and its by-product, over-consumption, one being the waste that it produces and the damage it continues to do to Earth. It was estimated that if all countries of the globe were to reach the standard of living that we in the global North live at now, five planets would be needed to get rid of the carbon emissions alone. As it is now, one third of arable land and tropical forests has been degraded, and one fourth of freshwater and one fourth of fish reserves have disappeared. This does not include the extinction of plant and animals. Current calculations suggest that we have exceeded the biosphere's capacity by over 50%. We are taking and taking without returning. We are damaging often irreparably, the very systems that brought us forth, that sustain us and that give us life. How is it that we cannot make the connection that any damage to these systems is damage to ourselves? If we pollute the water we drink polluted water, if we pollute the air we breathe polluted air, if we chop down trees and forests, not only do we increase the carbon monoxide in the air but we also deprive ourselves of hundreds of life-forms that each contribute to make the forest the unique and beautiful kingdom that it is. We deprive ourselves of the majesty of the oak and the pine who precede us by hundreds of years and all that they evoke in our spirit and our mind. Their beauty, their story, their significance. And we cut them down for what?

Not only does our consumption lead to a degradation of Earth but also to our humanity. This activity we have of continuously seeking to make life more luxurious, easier and more pleasurable has deadened us to the naked beauty of life that takes place around us at every minute. We don't need to elaborate on it or enhance it or adorn it. Life itself, in all its intricacies and dramatic moments is the beauty. And this is our poverty, the consumers, so blanketed and protected, it takes so much more for us to feel that we are alive. We have sugared over the very essence of existence. It is not enough for us when hot and sweaty from labour, a sharp breeze comes to cool us down; or sticky and befuddled, we take to the cool waters and the elements combine to make an adjustment in our own physical and mental well-being. Or when our body cannot contain our excitement and we feel that we shall burst unless we run fast and long and the freedom of that, of my own body carrying me, like an instrument, as natural as a bird might fly, or a fish might swim, is exhilarating. It is not enough for us to see the final raindrops after a storm, plump and full, as they plop unceremoniously onto the needles of the pine tree. Or to see the full moon bellowing in the night sky, bright and shining and wonderful casting light in all the places that night usually hides. The world has become insufficient for us because we no longer know how to participate in it. We would rather watch it take place through the window of our home or on the television screen, this primordial, elemental dance, than join in and be part of it, than to let ourselves be affected by it, to let ourselves get wet when it rains and be blown when it's windy, shiver when it snows. We don't join in and let ourselves be moved. We don't see or feel what is already here. We seem to always want more without experiencing what is here now.

But if someone has more, then someone by the laws of physics, has less. In this country we have prided ourselves on our generosity, on giving to 'people in need'. This has been done in different ways down through our history. We have produced missionaries and sent what spare money we had to them and their missions. We have continued this tradition by giving to International Aid agencies working to achieve poverty alleviation. But giving more money is never the answer. We must look at the lives we live ourselves, what we use and accumulate, what we throw away. There can never be poverty alleviation until we begin to make adjustments in our own ways of living. Our lifestyles and choices make people poor. It is one planet, we are one species and one person's greed is another person's hunger. Any diminishment of Earth is a diminishment of our very own selves. Would we accumulate and consume so easily and so thoughtlessly if we lived from the awareness that this planet, Earth, is finite, that she does not exist for our use and that we are a totally dependent part of her? Would we consume so easily if we realised how much it affects others? Would we consume so easily if we recognised the world as a living organism, as sacred and whole?

Every action has a reaction and a consequence. Wolfgang Sachs said it succinctly when he wrote it is not about giving more but taking less. Most of us have enough. Enough to live. Some of us have far too much. Some of us are just barely surviving. Those of us who can eat three meals a day have enough. Those who are barely surviving need their share which they cannot get if we take it. So the obligation begins in us, the privileged but impoverished of the global North to question again our desires and wants and what 'owning' something can afford us.

Abundance

In the time-developmental story of the Universe we learn that Earth is primary and that the human is a derivative of Earth, coming from natural processes and not superseding them. All our needs, physical and psychic come from this planet. Her fruits and vegetables feed us and her beauty arouses our spirit and our intellect, awakens our sense of wonder. This is our home, it is what is familiar to us and what we are intimately connected with. Here is where we experience life, not an interpretation of life but life itself, the same energy force that brought the world into being. Here is where we experience the Divine. Here is all we know. It has shaped our bodies, our sense of smell, our sense of touch. It has evoked the depth of feeling that creates poetry, the curiosity that invents science, the wisdom that inspires religion. It is not a resource or an object. It is our home.

This home is inhabited by over eight million different creatures, creatures that fly, creatures that swim, creatures that crawl. Each with its own unique beauty and role, fulfilling a niche that is only theirs to fulfil. Each a different colour, a different form, with a different voice, each with a different eye with which it gazes upon and interprets the world. Some of these creatures we can see with our own human eye, others remain imperceptible to us. This home is inhabited by mountains, by seas, by lakes, by forests, by deserts, by bogs. It is so full of every sound and colour and texture that we can imagine. In fact we cannot imagine beyond what Earth gives us to work with. It is her colour and sound that activates our own minds. This home is laden with fruits and berries and vegetables, with plants and herbs and trees. They reproduce and reproduce and pleasure our food with their scent and colour and taste. All we know is around us, filling the skies and rivers. And yet we live here as if this planet had no relation to our being, as if she is simply a background. And this, again, is our poverty.

We no longer listen to her speak or seek to communicate in any meaningful way with her. We no longer live in intimate presence with the birds who communicate in the language of the birds or the sea who communicates in the language of the sea or the mountains who communicate in the language of the mountains. The sacred is not present to us because we do not know how to recognise it, how to hear it, how to let it fill us. And this makes us poor. We crave an intimacy with the Divine but do not know how to communicate. We crave wealth and abundance but cannot see that what we have is enough. We desire to accumulate and possess but cannot recognise that nothing can ever be owned, not by any person because nothing is ours in the first place including our very own lives. It is one planet, one Universe, one timeless, seamless, travelling energy that is intimately connected and unfolding together. It is abundantly full and knows what is needed. We could not be here if we did not already have enough, we could not be sustained and continue to exist and to evolve if we did not already have enough. For most of us, our poverty begins in the mind and on the television, in our culture, but the world is far, far greater than human need and desire, and abundance is the characteristic that begins to be revealed as we open ourselves to life and how it is lived beyond us.

The Orange

All that it takes for an orange to grow. It takes the sun and the Earth working together. It takes the soil, the rain and the seed. Deep in the womb of the skies a series of inter-related activity that is hidden to the human eye until the orange appears on our tree. Its growth is so much deeper and dependent than what we give it credit for. What do we think when we eat that orange, an afterthought perhaps of our productive and generous sun working in relationship with Earth? What do we think when we unpeel its layers and its citrus scent is released into the atmosphere? Do we marvel at how it has come to be? Do we feel privileged by the fact that we can peel and eat it, indulge in its juicy sweetness? Do we wonder why it is that it is we who can appreciate it, who get to taste it? Are we grateful? Or do we simply eat it as if it was 'produced' for us, as if there will always be another, limitless and mine. A process began 93 million miles away, with so many elements and forces at work in its formation, do we really believe that it can be 'mine'?

There are other things in the world besides oranges. Things that also came about through deep, inter-related activity, such as the blossom of the Cherry tree, the high and low tides, the flow of the river and the birth of a child. Things that took the work of eons to emerge, that are present now, just as we are. Isn't that the ultimate symbol of wealth, existence? A culmination of activities that result in a human life, for however brief, for however bitter but a life that is born into a world that is intimately and deeply familiar to us, that left to her own devices will feed and clothe us, shelter us and sing to us. How could one be wealthier than that? If we knew what it took to be present, maybe we would never want more again?

Chapter 6
Love

Our ability to reflect on the world and on ourselves, to transcend our existence by asking what is this existence for, is, I have learned, a capacity that we have but remain unsure as to its purpose and how best to use it. Another capacity which we have but also remain unsure of how to carry it out, is the ability to love. The ironic nature of both these human capacities is that we do it regardless of our analysis of them, regardless of our commitment to them or our interpretation of them. They are innate in the human experience. We think and we love. For good or for bad. Love, as an idea and as an action, has captivated me both through personal experience and as a global aspiration. The womb of humanity, it births all that is most wonderful in us, calls us to greater ideals and greater expressions of ourselves, but often its lessons elude us.

Universal Love

The great religions and mystics teach about love and compassion and how if we are to become fully human that these capacities, most fully developed, are what we should aspire to. I see these as essential parts of our human nature which are at times more accentuated than others, which are at times provided more of an opportunity to show themselves than others, but that even when hidden remain at the core of what it means to be human nonetheless.

Teilhard in The Human Phenomenon writes that love is *"namely the affinity of one being for another....and is not unique to the human being"*[1]. In the same section entitled 'Love Energy' he writes :

> *Humanity, the spirit of the Earth, the synthesis*
> *of the individual and peoples, the paradoxical*

*reconciliation of the element and the whole, of unity
and multitude – for all these things, said to be so
utopian, yet which are so biologically necessary, to
actually take shape in the world, is not all we need to
do, to imagine that our power of loving develops until
it embraces the totality of men and women and of the
Earth?*2.

The beauty of this idea is that our power of loving can
develop and grow and become more, so that we too, can become
more. Teilhard believes that humanity is built for love. I believe it
too. I recently heard Brian Swimme say that there is no explicit
love reaching out from the Universe, that the love must come from
us, humanity as love manifest. In light of our recent history or
even the past fifty years, this is difficult to conceptualise – a
humanity that is distinguished by our ability to love. And yet, I
feel we would not have the ideals we have or the aspirations we
have, such as justice, peace and unity, even love itself, if we did
not have the potential to one day reach these aspirations and if
these ideals were not contained in some part of us already.

Some years ago as part of the Sophia Institute curriculum I
attended a workshop on massage so that on Holy Thursday I could
take part in a program where the feet of homeless people were
washed and massaged by volunteers - if they want. At first, I had
questions about this. Who has the right to massage somebody's
foot and why would anybody, homeless or otherwise, want to be
massaged by me? I also wondered whether or not this was some
subtle power thing where I could make myself feel better at the
cost and humiliation of somebody else – see how good I am to
come and massage your dirty, homeless foot – the kind of mixed
feelings where I was very curious but also apprehensive. It turned
out that for all my trepidation, my experience was humbling and
deep and stays with me still, not just because of the massage but
because of what happened that night.

It is a strange thing to take a stranger's foot in your lap, to wash it, dry it and massage it with cream. It is strange to focus completely on that foot as if it is the place where God most visibly resides. It is strange to run your hands along another's toes, between their toes and around their heel, ankle and instep. Your hand carving the shape of the foot, feeling the indentations and scars that life has left there, the bumps, the cuts, the nails, the decay. When we focus we can get lost in the body of another, in any part of that body, staring, touching, smelling. It is our human characteristic to be in awe of that which we walk around in ourselves. We are amazed by the body, even our own body. It is as if we cannot believe we have one. It is nearly as if it is separate from us and not actually us.

The purpose of the massage was not to focus on the man himself, his being without a home or what might have led to this, but to focus solely on his foot. In total that day I massaged seven pairs of feet, four men and three women. Five black and two white. All of these people were homeless. As we travelled home that evening, I could smell their feet on my hands and fingers. Every time I put my hand to my nose I could smell the feet that I had touched, a smell of stale sweat and heat. Rotting, withering flesh. It was nauseating and yet it was compelling. I could not stop putting my hand to my nostrils. I wanted to breath in that pungent, mixed smell of lives that were very different to mine; of people who stood outside the manufactured and watered over existence that we call society; whose feet and steps had lead them down a path where now there was little material comfort and where life was lived in its raw reality, unadorned and harsh but pumping through the hearts of these people and their ghost-ridden stories, making them real and mocking my concept of home. And yet there was a sadness too, sadness that we would let this happen to our own, sadness that we failed to protect, we and I and all of us who sleep under three layers of blankets with our two pillows and our bedside locker and lamp where we rest our mobile phone and our radio and alarm clock and the book that allows us not to think. I felt sad and envious at the same time but unable to reconcile how I could feel both ways, confused by which feeling I should act on and what these feelings were teaching me.

Later that night, along with others in my class I attended a Holy Thursday service in an Anglican church in Oakland where there was a Gospel choir singing. At a certain point in the service there were two bowls of water left in front of the altar. Two lines formed and every single person in that congregation came to have their feet washed. Feet. Again. Mothers washed their children's feet; father's washed their parents'; children washed their grandparents'; the old knelt down and washed the feet of the young and the young knelt down and washed the feet of the old. I felt it was a display of humility and service and love; a display of mutual need and goodness and hope, a desire to care for each other and nurture each other and recognition that we need to kneel before each other, before everything, not in submission but in gratitude and wonder at the life and being of another. We need to kneel in our searching ignorance before the mystery of it all, the mystery that is lived through another, without whom I could not be. We need to kneel because we do not know.

I thought back to my experience earlier that day and was humbled for the second time by people's ability to be open and to receive love, to be simple and unashamed about their need for it. Years ago I worked as a care assistant in a cancer hospital where my job was to bathe and shower the patients – the same thing struck me then as now. It is much easier to wash someone than to be washed myself, it is much easier to wash another's feet than to have another wash my feet. I wonder why this is and can only think that it is about pride and my reluctance to show myself as needing love, to show myself as weak and needy and vulnerable, as if anybody is not. Why is it discouraged to need others – is that not what makes us human and the belief that we are independent and individual that what has contributed to the mess that we are surrounded by today, to the idea of the human that is contrary to millions of years of wisdom – that we are separate, competitive, violent and dominating in our nature? I think that all we want to do is love, that we ache to love, to let it spill out of us and fill others up, to let it flow into us, warm us, breathe us until we can exhale it out again. That day, in the church and in that homeless centre, I saw people open up to others and open up to love, for what is love only being humble enough to receive and wise enough to serve and the realisation that we are all in this together, without better or worse only different? What is love - only something we receive so that we may pass it on? It is not ours to possess, but everybody's, passing through us, leaving us, returning, always present. Why have we made it so complicated and an aspiration when it is very much realised? Despite all our other questionable tendencies, we love just as much if not more than any other thing we do. We love in our helplessness and vulnerability, in the way we look at another, in how we breathe this precious breath we are given. We love not only in how we treat others but in how we let them treat us, when we let them take our dirty, calloused and aching foot in their lap and wash it, when we let them hold the fragility and brokenness and suffering that is part of life and for just one moment give them the opportunity to soothe it and let them experience the grace and compassion of wishing it were not so. We love in our silence and in our rage, in our confusion and hostility. We love because when we have exhausted ourselves trying to understand and rationalise this hazy existence, it is all that is left of us, the gentle current beneath every other emotion, thought and desire, the very breath of life itself.

A Personal Loss in Love

In our need to love, we seek out lovers and loved ones and anyone who will receive the abundance of it which cannot stay within us. It is the invisible thread from heart to heart holding people together, coming from the depths of us while at the same time revealing itself to us, inviting us to take part in its existence. Inviting us as if it had always been there, watching and waiting for our heart to be able to see and to respond. Coaxing and beguiling, beautiful and shining dancing from your beloved's eyes. See, I am the stars and the sea and everything else that came to be, looking deep within you, deep into the heart of you, the centre of you that you do not even know yourself. And the heart jumps for it knows that it is not the one who stands before you, who gently holds your hand and rests their forehead upon your brow, but the one who has always been, ancient, eternal and at that moment, passing through from the heart of one who is human, to the heart of you. Does it come upon us silently and suddenly changing everything like the quantum leaps of evolution, settling into our hearts, dis-arranging the plans and hopes we had lodged there and shaking the dust from our aspirations, inspiring us to be more, to be better? Do we know when it arrives – can we tell its coming, our anticipation prior to our knowledge, like the Earth waiting for rain, patient and sure, certain of its arrival? Why does it drive us so? What does it touch in us that we wish never to be without it?

In every heart there is regret. Something that lingers, dull and heavy and comfortable in its familiarity. It is a part that belongs to someone else; a part that someone did not take. It sits in the heart and it moulds it and shapes it. It is not bitterness or depression but the practical realisation that your greatest hope is not to be fulfilled. Even though it is your greatest hope, it is not to be fulfilled. Not ever. It is the realisation that all things are not possible, that people are not free and in life, for good or for bad, you do not always get what you most want. This is a strange knowledge to grapple with. If life is not about what you want, then what is it about? Whatever it is, I have come to know that it is not about me.

The thoughts I invested in this hope, the hours spent dreaming, over and over surrendering to the sweet pleasure of its temptation, lost in the beauty of the feeling that was unfolding from you. The joy in my anticipation growing from the depths of me like a prayer- my fresh heart singing for you, to you, uplifted and delighted. The tenderness you evoked in me surprises me still like a melting cloud drifting in a blue sky, awakening a beauty and sensitivity and gentleness towards everything. Gently, gently, afraid to hurt you, to hurt anything, afraid to breathe on this precious, fragile feeling. The softest, sweetest part of the heart and purest place of love, so tentative and new and slow to unfold. Curious and trusting it sought you out. But all people make decisions and you chose no. Is it still love even when you refused it? My days since have been the struggle to make sense of a world that is greater than a love that defined me - defined me and defied me, battered me and blinded me.

The thought of you can still flash across my mind – somebody walking with a gait similar to yours; a word, a gesture, a beautiful sunset or engaging conversation and there you are alive and present and beside me. So I tighten my stomach and clench my teeth and a steeliness rises from my gut and makes its way into my heart until I have pushed you from my head - the body is involved in this pain of the heart too, hardening itself against you. Those are the times when I am not happy to feel you, when the pain of your confusing and unskilled rejection is sharper than your loss. Other times I evoke you. Sinking deep into your memory, wanting to feel again the tenderness that you drew from me, wanting to feel the warmth of your smile, your smile for me, wanting to feel your eyes upon me with all their knowing, all their gentleness, full with all the words that you could never say to me. Could never and would never. I remember what it was like to lie beside you and how the whole world shrank to be the size of your bed, the size of you, curled and murmuring, your eyes closed listening to me talk and talk and talk, indulging me, a smile ever so slightly curling your lips. There was nothing else for me. There was nothing else I could have given you. There was nothing else I wanted and until you there had never been anything. I don't know why I felt what I felt or what was in you that lit me like nobody else has ever done. From the first time I saw you I just knew that if I got to speak to you that you would understand. Sometimes I didn't have to speak for you to understand. It was all there, palpable, the power of this unseen and unsaid feeling burning me up and bleeding me dry at the same time. But you never said anything and that was the most deafening no I have ever heard.

Do we love to different degrees? For such a curious species the harshest part of life can be that in our lifetime there are things that we will not know. I will never know what you felt for me, if your heart ever flickered or moved in response to mine. Some days I think probably not; other days I think that it would not be possible for me to feel what I felt if you felt nothing. But this love has given me one certainty – the heartache of its denial has grieved me and shown me how the deepest pain I have felt is the pain of the spirit – loss, grief, heartache. We can't see it but it is a wound that is concretely marked in us -invisible and untouchable but achingly present and gaping. It walks around with us and becomes part of who we are, speaking for us, thinking for us, understanding for us. I think of those whose loved ones have died and feel self-indulgent about my own dramatic response to loss and yet I cannot shake it free. I cannot shake you free. Can you heal something that human hands cannot touch?

What was it for, this love that was denied? What was its place among all the other loves that circle through our lives making it fleshy and sweet – the love of parent for child, of sister for sister, of teacher for student, the love of friendship. All of these loves helping to complete us, nurturing us. Why then does the rejection of one torment me? Perhaps it was mine to learn that 'want' and 'desire' are of the Universe and not of the person. Perhaps it was mine to learn that desire can never ultimately be fulfilled but lives in an anticipation that draws us forward all the time, towards different things and different people always ensuring its own existence, always desiring its own continuation, briefly satiated in the realization of an ideal that we have momentarily captured and which will eventually crumble as we realise its impossibility to be what we had hoped, to be what we had desired......and so the cycle continues and draws us to where we do not know but we know enough to follow it.

An Evolutionary Love

I briefly spent time in a Catholic convent as a postulant where I learned about and grappled with the notion of celibacy. I prefer to call it chastity as celibacy evokes a cold, cloistered and barren image of what the commitment entails rather than what it seeks to achieve. Ever since this time I have struggled with the notion of celibate love and have sought to understand if there is a way to love that is better than the rest, not better in a hierarchical sense but in a way that is more effective, that will bring about the fruits of love. Is there a way to love that is purer than others where each being is as Kant says 'an end in itself', and that raises human ideals?

There have been figures throughout history who have illustrated this love in the way that they lived their lives, people like Jesus Christ, the Buddha, Gandhi, Oscar Romero, Mother Teresa. Their lives were lived from the spirit, inspiring people to act and speak from the deepest place within them, to not forget that this life we live is one. They were lived in service, self-sacrifice and justice and were profoundly counter-cultural, even now, challenging people to use this life as a means to experience and know the Divine, as an opportunity to always seek God and whatever we do, to always try and do it in love. Their personal love was translated and infused with universal love. When I think back on my own experience, I have an inclination that the way I loved was not compatible with the love the Universe is seeking to develop, the love that must be for all. It could not be mine because it was not mine to have, it did not add to anything and it did not build anything. It was contained in and for one person and my own desire for that person. It did not spill over into the world but minimised it, reduced all my actions and all my thoughts to the altar of one person - selfish, self-centered and indulgent, ignoring the sacred gift that is in existence alone and that is sung by the seas and the oceans, by the plants and birds and trees. And yet, it also taught me that there is a well of love within me that I only need to be made aware of in order to draw from.

Can we love without desire and can we desire without love? I feel that it is desire that draws us forward revealing something to us that we have not yet named ourselves. It can take many forms but it is the same longing at the root. I do not know about celibacy but I recognise that we were not built to indulge all our desires nor to deny all of them. We are still a young species, overwhelmed by our body and repeatedly astounded by what it can do. We try to understand our desires, divide them into body and mind, good and bad, moralise about them. We say that it is because at heart we are animals, we say that the spirit is willing but that the flesh is weak and yet we do not try to understand why we desire in the first place and its connection to curiosity and exploration (other markedly human traits) or its part in coaxing us forward. Love, however, is not about exploration. It is the innate knowledge of something come to light in another, the human heart knowing already what the human mind and body are catching up to learn. Desire, in any form, is the wish to know and experience this love deeper.

In the Teilhard quote I used above he writes '*our power of loving develops until it embraces the totality of men and women and of the Earth'*. There is a connection between love and totality where the love of the many and the love of the Universe equate. Through the billions of years the Universe has been in existence, it has become more and more complex, its four basic building blocks (hydrogen, oxygen, carbon and nitrogen) complexifying. I have said it before but it needs to be repeated, we could not have stars without galaxies, nor planets without stars, nor life without planets, nor people without life. Growing and building through destruction and creation, death and birth, the arrangements of these four elements have eventually complexified into human beings and into our ability to love and take care of that which we are part of. I do not know how the primal peoples loved but there is evidence of caring through how they buried their dead and how they nourished their young and fed and hunted as a community. As society and 'civilisation' has become more complex perhaps our capacity to love has complexified also, calling us to an understanding of what love is about and what love is for or represents beyond simply 'caring'. What is the point of it with all its beauty and power and ability to hurt? If we believe that the Universe is intelligent and creative so we must believe that it has also created love and that it perhaps is aiming towards the love that is, as Teilhard wrote, the totality of all. Perhaps this is the love that transcends gender, race, nation and continent, that does not merely accept difference but that exalts in it, that does not only care about others but knows that 'I' do not exist without others. Perhaps it is the love that knows the sweetness and gift it is to be alive but realises that in one's own live are intermeshed and living the lives of many others. Perhaps it is the love that knows that denial is not death but a holding back of something that has not yet found its place. Perhaps it is the love that knows the person is here to serve the universal and although the Universe can often serve the person that people are not its final end nor to be indulged and pleasured as if a crowning achievement but merely a carrier of what needs to be expressed at this time in this place and through this manifestation. Perhaps it is the realization that in the fragmentary part of each person's, each creature's, existence, is the totality of all that has ever been, an existence which will eventually be consumed by the whole but leaving an indelible print on what the whole is. Perhaps it is the love that realises that it *is* love and wants everybody to taste it, to feel it and then to simply pass it on?

Chapter 7
Communication

In the twentieth century, quantum physicists discovered that within the smallest particle, there is a non-material realm. This is what is left when all matter is broken down. It is neither an energy constellation nor a material construct. It cannot be seen or measured. Scientists call this the quantum vacuum. Within this vacuum of pure space, elementary particles come in and out of existence, out of the vacuum itself. This 'empty', non-material realm is a place of pure generativity and is now believed to be the basis of material reality. Not only this, but quantum physics also revealed what is known as 'instantaneous action at a distance' also known as non-locality. This is the ability of paired particles who interact locally and then move far apart, to affect its pair at a distance without any immediate touch or force. It is their ability to communicate without any material or external force creating pressure.

As noted earlier, communion is one of the principles of this Universe. Everything that exists is characterised by this. Nothing can exist in isolation, being itself, a profound act of communion from the simple unquestioned act of eating, to the unremitting inhalation and exhalation of breath. These two examples of acts of communion, we do naturally and thoughtlessly. It is our desire to and practise of, communicating with each other, human to human that is more difficult as is our desire to communicate with that which we perceive to be of the Divine. With language, communication moves into the realm of consciousness and so enables the use of concepts and ideas which shape and deepen our communication. Through language we begin to articulate our reality and in doing so transcend our physical limitations. But we are long past language as a means of transcending our physical limitations, for communication, with the dawn of the Information Age has taken on an entirely new dimension.

Through digital and technological advancement, information has become easily available across the world. This access to information has changed the way we interact in the world. It has made the sharing of information between a girl in a city in Japan and a girl in a village in Ireland a possibility, without them ever having had to meet. The Information Age has seen the rapid growth of social media, in particular Facebook, where people can transmit information through photographs, posts, links and 'likes'. A glimpse at a person's Facebook page provides an overview of their lives. Or how they would wish their lives to be perceived.

Recently a video was posted on Youtube. It was of the execution by beheading of an American journalist by IS (Islamic State, formerly known as Islamic State of Iraq and the Levant). The execution with a prior spoken message by the executed to the American government, had been televised and posted on YouTube presumably within hours after it had taken place, and made immediately available for world view. Some days previously, an Australian Islamist State fighter had posted a photograph on his Twitter account of his seven year old son holding the severed head of a slain Syrian soldier. This photograph was also instantly accessible across the globe. Both of these images communicated information to the world. It struck me of the power of instant communication that the internet had established. But behind this instant access to information, there was no explanation of how it came to be, of what it might mean, of the story of the 'event' that we were able to witness. Just the information. Interpret it as you will. The images shocked me, a repulsive feature in sound and colour. Obviously, the purpose of these communications was to relay some form of information. But when does information become knowledge? And in communication of this type, it is singularly one-sided. Violent. An assault through image. There is no way open to the receiver to question or to respond.

As relational beings the way in which we communicate is vital. Process-relational philosopher Alfred North Whitehead, writes about relational power. This is an alternative to the view and exercise of power that has dominated down through the patriarchal, industrial age which is that of unilateral power. Unilateral power envisages power as "the ability to affect others without being affected by them." This power moves in one direction, from the top down. Whitehead, on the other hand highlights another form of power, a power that is just as active as the unilateral concept, and that is Relational Power. Mesle in his book on Whitehead writes that relational power has three components. These are:

1) *The ability to be actively open to and affected by the world around us;*

2) *The ability to create ourselves out of what we have taken in;*

3) *The ability to influence those around us by having first been affected by them* 1.

Relational power begins with the way in which we communicate. It is about first being open to others. Mesle doesn't differentiate here between human and other than human. He says it is about being open to *the world* around us and being affected by this world. This entails arriving at every communication without a prior agenda, of not filling the time until we can speak or express ourselves, but waiting to hear what is to be said. Open enough so that the words begin to mean something and that we take them in. If we do this we are inviting a change in our thoughts and our feelings, a change in who we are.

In that mysterious communication of the separated pair of photons, they both react simultaneously. We don't know yet why this happens, only that their connectedness and their relationship goes deeper than their physical and geographical association. If we use the Hermetic Principle of 'as above so below', then we can assume that our own relationships also go deeper than our physical and geographical association. Communication then could quite possibly begin even before we set eyes on someone or open our mouth. It could begin with a change in the flow of energy we receive or submit. This science is not new for many ancient cultures such as the Aborigines in Australia or the Celts of Ireland. It was intuited because they were far more open to the world than we are. We have had to learn through observational analysis and empirical testing that this is one of the ways in which the world works.

Jim Conlon taught about the many other modes of knowing, ways that have been supplanted by reason and rationality. Such modes are intuition, imagination, what we might call 'a gut feeling', dreams. Thomas Berry has also written that *"the effort to reduce all wisdom to a univocal language is a primary error or failure of our times"*[2]. Wisdom comes through experience and our experience comes through our relationality, in short, our ability to communicate. It does not come through language or knowledge but openness to the world so that we are aware at some level of a change in being.

Do we need to see Youtube videos' of beheadings and Twitter photographs of heads as trophies to be told that there is something drastic and violently wrong with the way in which we communicate as a species? What are we trying to proclaim? That there is a greater race amongst this one species, that there is a greater God, a greater ideology, something that justifies profanities like these, something that we can learn from these acts? These acts, as their subsequent communications, are unilateral. The antithesis of how the world works. The human in disaccord, acting unnaturally lost in layers and layers of miscommunication. If that soldier had had time to think, to close his eyes and let himself be affected by his captive, had the strength to let himself be affected, could he have still slit his throat with a knife?

Underneath his religion, underneath the colour of his skin, there are his cells, without which he could not claim a religion. In these cells are his atoms. When these atoms are broken down, there exists that non-material dimension to reality, what Brian Swimme calls the fecund emptiness, or the 'Widely Dispersed Unitary Event', the seamlessness of life that connects that soldier to the man he will murder. Why could he not feel it? What blocked him? If he had communicated with his entire body, could he have felt it then? And then to pass on his own blocked, violent communication, perpetuating over and over again that initial act on film. This man shows no signs of malleability, no openness, only his own desire to spread his own message in a forum that makes it increasingly easy to do so.

Youtube does not tell us what has brought him to this point, nor Facebook reveal the taunts, disappointments or struggles that may have led to his hardening. All we see are the end results. And this is when communication becomes a problem, we encounter an end result and the action of it creates our own hardening. Thomas Berry's words echo out a warning - we do not know where we are in time and space except for the story of events that have taken place. Communication is about story. The exchange of story, the freedom to tell it, the ability to receive it deeply into our own selves and to be changed by it.

The more we are absorbed into the actualisation of our own lives and desires the less effective we are in our communication with the world. Poet Coleman Barks wrote that *"this is the material plane and every outward thing we do is inner work"*3. I wonder did he know about the non-material plane of reality. I wonder did he know that communication begins deep in the recesses of our own selves, in our intention and our attention, in how we are present to and in the world. Being a poet, he probably does. For poetry is another way to know the world. Jim once wrote when we write or read a poem *"we gain access to what is imaginative, intuitive and a deeper source of wisdom than the mind can discern, express or understand "*4. It is a way to let the world come to us on its own terms.

With technology, people have begun to communicate in a way where relationship is unnecessary, where they do not have to account for themselves or engage in a gradual building of shared story and trust. Put up a picture, post a message, like a photograph. It is a cheapening of reality, a reality and a relationality that people do not have to work at. All of the information without any of the meaning. It is time to realise that the outside is only some of what we are, that reality begins in our own hearts and dreams and imaginings and hopes. To establish a true communion amongst ourselves, the self-reflective element of this Universe, our communication must have meaning and depth, must begin in a sensitivity to the seamlessness of life and the realities that are wrought from there. Prayer is another way to do this, not prayer in the sense of petition but prayer as a means of communication. Again, in the words of Jim prayer as "*an enhanced awareness of the ocean of sacredness that life offers, a greater capacity to notice the ebb and flow of existence*"5. This primordial desire to connect to the energy and flow of life is within us all, to connect to it and to communicate it, to pass it on. It cannot be done through technology, nor ideology, it is released in our personal relationship with the world, with each other and in our ability to be in tune to that in-dwelling realm of spaciousness, that quantum vacuum that connects us all.

Chapter 8
Friendship and Joy

Natural selection is one of the determining processes of how evolution works. It works from the premise that whatever traits, anatomically and physiologically, are beneficial to our survival and reproduction, will be maintained or selected and those that are not will be eliminated or pass out of existence by virtue of the fact that they are not beneficial. It is a process by which living organisms adapt in order to survive life in their environment. In his book 'The Social Conquest of Earth', American Biologist E. O. Wilson puts forward the theory that human nature may also be an evolutionary consequence. He writes *"human nature is the inherited regularities of mental development common to our species. They are the 'epigenetic rules' which co-evolved by the interaction of genetic and cultural evolution that occurred over a long period in deep history"*[1]. These behaviours, Wilson goes on to say, are not hardwired but are learned. This is the theory of gene-culture evolution where because of both genetic and cultural pressures, we evolve with specific traits because they contain some kind of social or evolutionary advantage.

This information, that human nature and the universal characteristics that we share may also be an evolutionary development, has made me think again about some of our shared human traits, traits that transcend language, race and culture. Two such traits are the human propensity to friendship and the human propensity to joy. Friendship is a relationship, while joy is a response, a response to how we relate. Both are pleasures, pleasures that are freely given. Although these pleasures are given, the fact that they have developed, are desired, and remain as identifiably positive experiences, would suggest that perhaps they have a benefit to society. Does our pursuit of them and the effect they create on us contribute to a society and indeed a world that is a certain way which it would not be if these two aspects were absent? Their continued presence and our attraction to them suggests that maybe friendship and joy have a deeper and more purposeful presence than simply the pleasure they elicit.

Friendship

Thomas Berry tells us that in the Confucian tradition, the human is the microphase of the cosmos and the cosmos is the macrophase of the human; that each discovers itself and is revealed through the other. This gives huge importance to the human as it infers that the cosmos is the larger dimension of the individual with the individual conversely containing the qualities of the cosmos. As a result, the moral and spiritual development of the human was of primary importance, and this development took place in community, through personal and social discipline. In Confucianism, the fundamental law of community existence was the sharing of joy and sorrow and because of this, friendship and the role it plays in human development, played a huge part. Berry writes:

> *This friendship community is, however, most important in fostering some of the deepest of all human experiences precisely because it is neither ritualised, not politicised, nor intellectualised, not subject to family obligation. It belongs to the order of the greatest freedom and creates a unique intimacy of its own. It is simply that attachment that individual persons and small groups of persons have for each other and the joy they have in their sharing of life and thought and feeling.*[2]

Friendship, as Berry says, is in its essence an example of the attraction of beings for each other. It is not enforced or obliged but rather it is the mutual choice and desire to be close. Within its bonds we express ourselves as fully and as freely as we can while at the same time permitting someone else to do the same. Through our ability to be vulnerable we allow another to be vulnerable, through our ability to listen we allow another to speak, through our ability to be honest, we allow another to be free. It is the arena wherein we most directly see the results of our own behaviour. There is an imperative in deep relationship, as in friendship, where we are consistently invited to respond to 'the other'. This is a position of responsibility and authority that has been conferred on someone through trust. Because of this gesture of trust, we are bound to look at our responses, to self-examination in order that we 'do right' by the one who has made the decision to invite us into the sharing of their being. A privilege by any stretch of the imagination. In order that we honour this privilege, we act from the interests of the other. The way in which we act is told in how the friendship develops.

In his book Walden, Thoreau writes "*What sort of space is that which separates a man from his fellows and makes him solitary? I have found that no exertion of the legs can bring two minds much nearer to one another*"3. Confucius writes about how friendship in its most authentic form, is a spiritual exercise. As Thoreau suggests, it is an intimacy of mind and spirit which goes beyond physical proximity. It is precisely because of this that it is a factor in our spiritual and moral development. It is the ground through which we negotiate the world with another, agenda free. It is where we learn to value someone for what they are themselves rather than what they will afford us. In friendship we work out our assumptions, our biases, our ideas of perfection, even our knowledge. It challenges us in the way we love and to what extent we will let someone affect us. It challenges us in our ability to forgive. It is fundamentally a sharing of one's life from the inside out.

There is too in friendship a joy that is released effortlessly, born of the freedom that friendship affords, the freedom to be oneself. It comes with unthreatening delight in each other's company, where we are permitted to play. To throw our head back in abandon and laugh must be one of the sweetest pleasures of life itself. Even the sound of laughter is pleasurable, a sound that penetrates a thousand languages. In this act, or reaction, a world of worry can be wiped away and the world and the mind are made fresh and twinkling again. Its effect on us as great as sleep. It energises us and opens our heart, makes us warmer, more receptive, makes us softer. Friendship evoking joy and joy helping us to be part of the world in a specific way, in a way that is more benevolent and in a way that is kinder.

Joy

Political activist Emma Goldman famously once stated about the anarchist revolution, that if she couldn't dance then she didn't want to be a part of it. There are times that I feel that way about life, that there is no point in participating unless it is with joy. What if we were to imagine a world that is joyless, no laughter, no smiley eyes, no spontaneous uncensored outbursts. I wonder if I could be part of a world like that. I imagine it to be like a wet blanket, stark and grey and drab. Serious and severe.

Teilhard de Chardin writes about the "zest for life" and about the importance it plays in activating our energy. It is this zest for life that enables us to rise to life's challenges. According to Teilhard it is a spiritual energy and is activated by wonder and awe. I feel it is also activated by joy, by the ability to be moved innocently and naturally by life's beauty and dramas. When we are joyful, there is an energy that rises in us. It is as if momentarily, the gateway to the benevolence of the Universe has opened up within us and come rushing through, where suddenly we are burst open and electrified by the world. Our heart and mind expanded. Amazingly, the things that can do this are small. They are free. Roses in full bloom, a smile, a memory, a conversation. The sun. The rain. It is our response to these that can be large.

To be joyful requires a certain degree of surrender and letting go. My former teacher, Jim Conlon writes of how letting go and letting be are the hardest spiritual practises, but if we can do well what we are able to do and then surrender what we have done with trust, that there is a great freedom in this, and with freedom comes joy. It is strange how freedom also evokes joy. Freedom in this sense being that although we have responsibility we are not singularly responsible, that although we have an obligation to act, that we can only do what is within our capacity to do. There are many worries in the world, many problems and tragedies, many things that if we care about the world we should fight about. Serious issues like climate change, like the consistent and rising violence in the Middle East, famine and hunger, poverty, gangland wars. There is an urgency to these problems that by virtue of our shared ancestry and our shared future, we are obliged to act on. But the fight against these problems should not be one that makes us bitter or cynical. The world is not enhanced by either of these, rather it is diminished and belittled. If we are bitter or cynical, I ask that we consult again what we spend our time thinking and dreaming about, what we spend our time doing, and change them. I don't know if one person can change an imperfection in her life time but I do know that we all, each of us, make a contribution. Cynicism is not a worthy one. It is the act of one who thinks they have seen it all, who refuses to be surprised, who refuses to be inspired. It does not build but reduces, reduces the life of the one who is cynical and reduces the world to the way in which she believes it to work.

The world is a work in progress. It can make us weary because it does not bend to us. We, our very own species, maybe even our very own person, are responsible for so many of its afflictions and yet the resilience of life and its unbridled joy keeps on rising up in the most unexpected of places. It continues to bloom. It continues to play. Joy touches into the heartbeat and energy, the very pulse and flow of life. A force that involves us, that participates through us, a force travelling for billions of years. This energy exalts and comes alive in unity, in community, in the opening up to 'the other'. Joy transforms us physically and mentally. It is fleeting but its power is such that the momentum of the feeling can reside even after it has passed. On the back of joy, we become alive, smiling and beaming and revelling in the world.

Together…..
Although not immediately obvious, I believe that there is a connection between friendship and joy, a connection other than that friendship creates joy. This connection is that their existence is deeper than the pleasure they evoke. They are examples of a coax. Their sweet pleasures an enticement towards a more relational, kinder world. One a relationship, the other a response. In friendship we are given the opportunity to better our own nature under the loving, compassionate gaze of another. It is a relationship where if one grows, the relationship grows so that any growth, any insight learned or compassion practised will enhance that relationship, not just the individual. It is a learning that occurs at the level of being, the level of spirit and is then brought beyond that relationship into the wider community so that all can benefit. It is one of our first tests of compromise, glimpses of compassion, feelings of care. It is the seed where we begin to build society. To have a just, honest, compassionate world, one must first learn to become a just, honest, compassionate person. The way to do that is to be a friend, a friend in the understanding of Confucius. The gift of friendship has been given us as an opportunity to learn and to experience what life could be like. We strive for an ideal of perfection without realising that this is what we are striving towards. We work for this relationship out of love. We are shown how deeply we can care. The human is the microphase of the cosmos and the cosmos is the macrophase of the human. In one person, one relationship, we are loving the entire Universe. Through one person, one relationship, we are the Universe trying to perfect itself. Can there be a more pleasurable way to grow?

Joy on the contrary is not a way we learn. Its benefit lies in the effect it has upon us. The effects I mention above such as openheartedness, kindness, benevolency. Joy lights us up, lights the world up, imbues us unthinkingly with a sense of hope and a sense of excitement. The most marvellous part about it though is that we pass it on. We experience it and pass it on. To feel joyful is to feel alive, to feel fleetingly the force of the Universe and to know, in whatever knowledge is, that these moments alone, are worth the journey. Joy builds our capacity of perseverance.

In many ways, although affected by culture and genetics, life remains a choice. The epigenetic rules are learned and not hardwired and what is learned can be unlearned. Fortunately, some choices are made easier because of their affects, the benefit of having a friend, the benefit of being joyful, and the grim and severe alternative reality without them, is one that is sobering and deterring. And so, I wonder, does the Universe works its magic in an enticing and alluring way by allowing us to choose what is better, by allowing us to build what is good or are these accidental sweetness' of life that make us grow unwittingly?

Chapter 9
Violence and Evil

Conscious and loving though our Universe may be perceived to be, there is also something dark and ambivalent contained within it, something ambiguous which seems to be integral to its development. It is a creation marked by destruction from the beginning. The beginning as we know it, in so much as anything has a beginning, an explosion. It must have been loud and fierce, emitting light and particles, scattering its foetus across the dark and violently becoming the space and time it was simultaneously creating – could that have been peaceful? Particles colliding and perishing, their existence bright, brief and then death. A spectacular unfolding, *the* most spectacular unfolding, equal parts beauty and creation, equal parts violence and destruction, not for human eyes but in it the seed from which human eyes would come. So much has happened, so much time passed and so many monumental transformations before we could turn a human eye upon them. What would have happened if we were explicitly there at 'the beginning', if we had seen the Universe breathe itself into existence, watched its magnificence and precision up close, watched the intelligence that we try to comprehend by naming it creative and destructive, by naming it violent and beautiful, by naming it intelligence. It is beyond our comprehension even though that very moment or event (how do we classify the beginning of time?) is contained in everything including the human species. The darkness, the ambivalence, the contradictions, this destruction is all contained in us too.

Energy, Resistance and Dreams

One of the principles of the Universe that has captured my imagination because in some way it speaks to this concept of destruction and violence, is how the Universe is founded on

Energy, Resistance and Dreams, which Brian Swimme also calls Past, Present and Future. The dynamic of resistance indicates the privilege that it is to exist. All things resist and fight against the reduction of their presence in the world including the smallest particles. We feel inherently and innately our own value and contribution to this story. That is why day after day people choose to get up and live through the most 'dismal' circumstances. There is something innate in us where we feel the privilege of what it is to be part of this 13.8 billion year story. We feel the sacredness of it, the gift it is. It is this continued desire to exist that can contribute to the violence and the suffering that are part of this great adventure. The Pauli Principle states that no two particles can occupy the same place at the same time - if it is you then it cannot be me. It sounds so simple and yet we react so strongly to it. We feel the need to prove ourselves, to be the best, the one who endures. Competition has become a deeply ingrained mode of being in the human psyche, and yet are we ever competing against anyone but ourselves? And even if it is you, is it not also me? Are we not one and the same? Does the Universe not act as a whole? These questions are easier to ask than to answer but they come from the part of us that grapples with suffering and loss, the part of us that wishes it wasn't so but even still in our own way, perhaps unknowingly, are a contributing factor to both suffering and violence.

We need go no further than our own heart and examine our own actions and motivations to illustrate the limits of the human condition. There remains a gap between what we aspire to, what our deepest intentions are and the practical realisation of who we are. How does it happen that we build and detonate bombs, with no other intention than to kill and to destroy- burning villages, burning people, burning animals until there is nothing left but the scorched and burning Earth? How does it happen that nations who are superficially divided by tribe or by religion turn on themselves and try to purge the country of all those whom they perceive to be different from them? Or that a girl of seventeen years who happens to be an only child, arrives in Ireland on an International Student Exchange programme and is raped and murdered on her second night in the country by somebody whom until that time she has never known existed? Or that two boys both aged ten years, take another young boy, aged two years, and walk him two miles to his death, torturing and eventually killing him in the most brutal and grotesque way causing a frenzy in England about its decline in moral values? Or that a husband can beat his wife? Or that a teacher seduces the ten year old boy in her class? Or that we hunt whale and elephant and dolphin to fuel the growing 'needs' of our consumerist world? Or that we dump toxic waste into our oceans killing thousands of life forms there as equally precious to this planet as we are? Or that we demolish the forests and pull apart the land, mine it so that we can wear gold watches and diamond ear-rings; poison the seas so that we can drive cars? How can this be a loving and thoughtful Universe when we are capable of and commit such atrocities?

Is there Evil?

These human behaviours must not be confused with the destruction that is such an intrinsic working part of our Universe. They differ because they are not sacrificial. Nothing is born of them, they are an end in themselves, death for death's sake, without the promise of anything to come. Man–made. On the other hand, our tsunami's, Earthquakes and volcanoes are processes which regulate our planet, a way in which Earth self-organises. The violence of the supernova explosion a way in which the Universe creates, such death an example of the Universe mid-transformation. This violence and destruction a sacrifice towards the whole.

All of the human acts I mentioned above, however, would seem to indicate something contrary to growth and harmony, something contrary to life. In Christianity this force has been called evil. But is it enough to call it 'evil'? Should we just hand over our quest to understand these acts to the label of 'evil' and place it alongside all the other conquests of evil throughout human history that still baffle us? Or should we seek to understand these actions more and how they might differ from the violence and destruction that seem to be an integral part of the Universe?

It seems to me that 'evil' cannot exist outside of us but must be part of the whole and an intrinsic part at that, existing from the beginning. Teilhard writes *"nothing could ever burst to light in the world as final one day........if it has not existed at first in some obscure primordial way"*[1]. It is the same with consciousness, it could not just simply arrive, dropped into the world suddenly from outside it. This capacity in some form must always have been present. I do not want to reduce what is stark and extremely hurtful on so many levels by saying that because it might have always been here that it is legitimate and has a place but I do want to say that perhaps the language we use in our effort to understand it has not been helpful. Nor does our present understanding of the human as the crowning glory of life help either, or the fact that our ethics and morality so often begin with and end with the human only and do not take into account the created whole and the hundreds of thousands of other beings we share the Earth with, including Earth herself. There are, and have been, unequivocally, events that go fundamentally against life, such as those I mentioned above. Events that bewilder and pain us. But to reduce them to a force called evil can take away both our collective and individual responsibility for these happenings. It can also free us from having to think in any deep or meaningful way about the way that our societies, lives and relationships are structured; our relationships with Earth, with each other and with that which we deem to be sacred. It may even go so far as preventing us from engaging with what we think life is for and how we imagine the sacred to be. This is why it is important to question such concepts as destruction and evil in light of what we are learning now about how the Universe works.

So what might be some of the factors that lead us to act in such horrific ways?

The Disconnected Human

Thomas Berry writes that we have lost touch with the natural world at a very fundamental level. Diarmuid O Murchu writes that humanity gets it right, not perfect, but right, for most of our time here on Earth when we remain close to nature. It is when we lose our place in the natural order of things, when we don't see ourselves as part but see ourselves as whole that we act in deviant ways. He writes:

> ...for most of our time here on Earth, we behaved as an innovative, creative species. For most of that time, we got it right! As a creatively wise species we will always get it right rather than wrong, provided we remain close to the Earth in which we are grounded and attuned to the cosmos to which we belong. Over the past eight thousand years of patriarchal domination we have not fared well. This has been one of our dark ages, and the massacre of 62 million civilians in the wars of the twentieth century amply verifies this. But eight thousand years is less than 1 percent of our entire story, and in all probability it is not the only time in which things went badly for humanity......will we forgive ourselves, outgrow this dysfunctional way of behaving, and opt to become a cosmic-planetary species once more?"[2]

Similarly, Thomas Berry has written that there is a radical discontinuity between the human and the natural world and that we have become autistic in our relationship with Earth. The modern human has been in existence for an estimated 200,000 years but our fractured relationship with Earth began only when we began to manipulate her for our own benefit through means of agriculture and animal taming. Fossil records and other relics of this period show that this probably first began around 12,000 BCE. This is, as Diarmuid writes, a fraction of the time we have been alive. But since then we have managed to separate ourselves at a very essential level from the natural world. Most of the world's population live in cities or towns, amidst the noises as well as the pollution such over-populated places produce. There are, without exaggeration, people who have never seen the sea or been in a field. There are people who have never witnessed animals grazing naturally. This would have been an unimaginable and impossible fact less than five thousand years ago. We now know that we are shaped by the natural world, not just our body and how we move through the world, but also our interiority, our spirituality. What do living conditions such as these do to the human psyche? Does concrete make us harder and sky-rises make us feel invincible? How can we be nourished by our home if we build and tarmac over her and drown out all her other species? How can we know who we are if we do not know where we are from, what feeds us, and what we need to be nourished?

Thomas Berry has written that all our physical as well as our psychic nourishment comes from the natural world. How could it not if we come from it ourselves? So what are we doing to ourselves, to our own human psyche, to our understanding of ourselves and our place in the world when we damage and destroy the very natural processes that we are?

As a result of this disconnection we do not seem to realise that just as we are in the Universe, that the Universe is in us. That just as we are on Earth, that we are *part* of Earth's processes and cannot exist independently of her. Earth is not separate from us. What happens to the interior who has forgotten this, who sees the world, the planet we live on, as a 'thing', a resource. From where and what does their sense of belonging come? How do they orient themselves into life's cycles? Is it unfair to suggest that deviant behaviour is a consequence of this separation and disconnection?

If we do not see ourselves as connected or related to the world around us then it is easy to harm, to harm even without believing it to be harm. If we grow up in a world where birdsong is not revered or even heard, where trees are no different or no more valuable than a street lamp, where our surroundings are largely concrete, steel and plastic, where we move from house to car to office, our engagement with the living breathing world is diminished and so as a consequence, being a biological species who emerged from biological Earth, we too are diminished. There is nothing to stir our own organic hearts, none or very little of the spirit that is the natural world to light us up so that we feel this connection. This insularisation of life, the housing and manufacturing off it so to speak, is detrimental because it facilitates separation and disconnection. In this closeted world through television, radio, the internet, we choose what we will engage with and so we choose what will form us; we choose what will nourish us and we choose how we will occupy our time and what will fill our thoughts, instead of being exposed to the natural world and letting that form us. Life becomes to be interpreted and actualised by my own understanding and desire of what it should be rather than having a direct uncensored exposure and experience of what it is; value becomes something that's bestowed on others through my own values and experience rather than others having their own innate value. All this contributes to producing an exalted sense of self, the illusion that life is only what affects me. It is my view that this can contribute to stunted personal and spiritual growth, to behaviour which is detrimental to myself and to others, to a distortion of what is real and so as a result, deviant and harmful acts.

Time

Not only has this radical discontinuity between the human and the natural world led to diminishing human behaviours but it has also led to a dysfunctional relationship with time based on the view that time exists independently of this Universe and independently of our own lives, which in turn contributes to such diminished behaviour.

I was very privileged to be able to spend some time working and studying at Genesis Farm with Miriam Therese

MacGillis. My memories of that wonderful farm situated in the Appalachian Ridge, are of an area that was teeming with life, bursting with it, as if Miriam and all her companions throughout their thirty year presence had loved the land right back into being. There was an abundance of butterflies, insects, bees, birds, even black bears, and in the night the stars seemed to sprinkle down their blessing, shining brighter in approval of what was being accomplished there. But aside from the beauty and simplicity of that remarkably healthy place, Miriam also taught me about our time-developmental Universe. One of the topics she spoke on was deep time, a concept that has yet to fully infiltrate how we view the world.

Deep time is an understanding of time which initially included the age of Earth, making it geological, but now is extended to include the age of the Universe. It reveals how young we, the human being, is and tries to orient us into just how old the Universe is, how many things have come before us and how our coming to be was so dependent on all these events that preceded us. To think in deep time means to think cosmically and not just in the history of the Human or the history of Earth but in the history of the Universe. It illustrates how bound into the entire history of the cosmos we are with the primordial hydrogen in the water in our bodies and the iron in our blood created in the stars. Our eye in order to see uses a remodelled chlorophyll molecule developed by the early micro-organisms while our vertebra was developed 510 million years ago. And this is deep time, the acknowledgement of the seamlessness of creation, how one event leads to another, and how all of past time, of evolution, is in some way contained in our very own body.

Related to this is the equally important concept of deep vision. Because we more often than not, do not realise the age of Earth, of ourselves and how it took all that was to bring us forth, we have lost our sense of deep vision. We don't see what is there before us but rather we see in a limited and superficial way. We see trees as lumber, mountains as uranium, bogs as fuel sources without realising that they predate us, that they shaped us. Earth has become a resource, not something to be communed with or to be intimate with or to learn from. Because we don't know this story, this big history of how things have come to be, we live in a mechanical and functional way and our time has come to be measured, and more frighteningly, executed, by a machine. We have divided time into segments in an effort to be more productive and efficient. And so, for most people, particularly those of us in the 'developed' industrial North, at nine o clock we go to work, at eleven o clock we have a break, at five o' clock we go home and at the weekend we rest. Thomas Merton once wrote and I echo his sentiments 'what *is* 4 o'clock?' These numbers are meaningless and yet the clock and this understanding of time, a result of the industrial-economic era, dictate largely how we spend our quota of energy here on this planet, in this body. They dictate how we think and how we arrange and plan our lives. The clock divides the human being into parts, reducing us into compartments of work, rest, exercise and social time. This division separates us further from any natural and holistic sense of being and leaves no opportunity for us to experience time, to let it come through us.

But time begins to take on a different dimension when it is understood within the context of the Universe. When we refer to the age of the Universe, we use a scale of billions of years. These numbers are immense and for me at least, extremely difficult to relate to. A billion is not something I can conceptualize. But from the very enormity of these numbers and with the help of the concept of deep time, I am able to deduce three things. These are:

1) That the Universe is –in human measurement – incomprehensibly old. It is an ancient entity in so much as we, with our new human minds can comprehend what ancient is; and we, the human being are extremely new.

2) It takes a long time for things to evolve either chemically or biologically and that evolution is a

painstakingly slow process (I am not referring here to cultural evolution) and finally,

3) Time cannot be fully understood by the way we measure it today, that is, by the clock. This is reductionist, misleading and inadequate. It is a human measurement of something that contains the human but that is not human.

The entire concept of time is reprioritized and expanded when looked at from the cosmic view. It ceases to be about days or hours but becomes instead to represent what emerges and what is created. Brian Swimme talks about the time for hydrogen, the time for galaxies, the time for Earth, the time for consciousness. We now know that our Universe develops through time. It is not mechanistic or fixed but that it creatively develops; that it is not a place or an object but an emergent process, unfolding in time and through time, marked by those moments of transformation. Time in this sense then is about the emergence of what is new, of what has not happened or been before. Time becomes the manifestation of creative events. Encapsulated under this term of creative event are all beings including the human, as well as what each being themselves creates, creation here being what comes uniquely from the depth of an individual. Einstein once wrote that time is the space between events, and again taken in this context, time becomes about the creation process and how something gestates and prepares before it can be born so that the emphasis is not on the in-between space, such as the hours, days, years or months it may take to do this, but on the creative event itself. On its development and its birth. This view of time reduces the clock to insignificance as the priority becomes instead on what is needed to birth this idea and this cannot be reduced into thinking in days or hours because creativity requires a larger trajectory. We cannot produce anything meaningful, anything authentic on demand, especially if that demand is in a divisive time frame. Instead, we need the time it takes to access the energy needed to create. We are each of us our own time, trying to connect with and relate to the world in a meaningful way, trying to understand what is required of us by being here. This necessitates an insertion into the energies of the Universe which we most directly activate through our relationship with the natural world, that part of the Universe that is most intimate and accessible to us. How can I connect to the bigger event that is this cosmic unfolding, trying to do so by measuring time on a machine, a machine that was made by man? How can I connect to the bigger event if I am disconnected from the Earth?

Connected to this is the realization that, as Thomas Berry and Brian Swimme also tell us, each event is irreversible and non-repeatable. It cannot be repeated and it cannot be undone. This solar system a unique event never to be repeated, our Earth a unique event never to be repeated. Each person is a unique event never to be repeated. All that we do, all that we say, all that we create cannot be undone but becomes part of the very fabric of the cosmos itself mixing with all that is and changing it. Doesn't that give us huge responsibility? Doesn't that make our lives and how we choose to use them hugely important? Doesn't it change the very nature of what it means to be alive?

We have, most of us, in the past one hundred years, slipped out of the sacred presence of our planet. We have slipped out of the sense of time as being about emergence, as coming through us. We don't see it in its spiritual dimension, as becoming more complex, more diverse, more beautiful, more alive. We have reduced it to something that can be measured and divided, that can be 'spent'. Thomas Berry and Brian Swimme have written of how the obligation of each generation of beings is to attend to the creativity inherent in the moment. In order to do this then, the most important question a person can ask is, what time is it? What time is it in the Universe? What time is it in the unfolding dynamics of Earth? What time is it in the human story? Whose time is it to be created? Time in this sense is the whole. It is the entire evolution, the entire journey where right now, we are playing a part. It is our time and how we live now will condition what will come next. This epic is much, much greater than a twenty-four hour clock. It is told in seasons, in happenings, in anticipations, in ages and eons. It is told in past events, past peoples, past places. Our own individual lives are also much greater than this clock, much more important than the commercial and economic lives we assign for ourselves. We are cosmological beings, brought forward by the stars and moulded by the Earth. Commerce, industry and politics are all secondary. Time is about dipping into our cosmic heritage, combining who we are now with all that went before so that our actions can bring forth something even greater again.

Knowing our Story

I am sure that there are other factors that lead to our destructive and dysfunctional behaviours, but believe that the two mentioned above are fundamental in how we orient our lives within the natural order. They are responsible for whether we flow with the creative urge of the Universe or whether we flow against it. Our disconnected and out of synch psyche, our bodies starved for air, for freshness, for life, our whole system that is chained to and executed by a twenty four hour clock, all these factors contribute to alienate people in their humanity until they feel that to be human itself is not a natural expression of Earth and of the Universe. Popular psychology talks about how the human rages against the human condition and our own limitations and perhaps we do. But perhaps the reason we do is because we have drowned out all the species, the trees, the flowers, the other beings of this planet that teach us what to be human is, that teach us how to be human.

The human being is limited, anything that exists is limited. Our limits are set because as the Universe unfolds so too are we unfolding, incomplete, young, foolish and dizzy with all that we have been given. Overwhelmed by the abundance of life and overwhelmed by our own powers and capabilities to manipulate it.

And manipulate it we have, we have made mistake after mistake trying to understand ourselves and the great cosmos that we are part of, trying to understand our role, the way that we should be, what we should do, trying to understand what it means to be alive, and afraid to at the same time. But we will never understand who we are until we know where we come from, until we know our history and this greater story of how we came to be. Thomas Berry has written that *"there is eventually only one story, the story of the Universe. Every form of being is integral with this comprehensive story."*3. We ignore our history at our peril. It is my view that it is time to learn this story so that we may know who we are and act accordingly.

Chapter 10
Authenticity

In the beginning of his series, Cosmos, Carl Sagan says that *"we wish to pursue the truth no matter where it leads"*1. It must have been this kind of a sentiment that drove Galileo, Einstein, and all those other night sky watchers when they realised through their observations that it takes time for light to travel through space. Their uncompromising intellect enabling us to state now, that at night, when the Earth has turned her back to the sun, and our eyes are captured by the stars that are spread across the heavens that we are in fact, face to face with the past. Such a fact, even to this day, is difficult to fathom, and yet according to Sagan, we must have the integrity, both intellectual and personal, to follow where it brings us.

To look at a star is to look at a moment of history. A moment that is over. Duncan says when writing about this phenomenon that we don't see stars as they are now, *"rather we see them as they were when the light left them"*2. The star may not even be in the same place now as when the light left. We know that light travels at 300,000km per second and depending on when the light left that star and how far away the star is, the time it takes for the light to reach Earth will vary. What this information teaches us is that the past can be present in an immediate and observable way to us. To pursue the truth of this is to be brought into the workings of this Universe, into its intricacies, its inter-relatedness, into our own concepts and assumptions about time. It is to engage with the fact that there exists activity in the Universe beyond our own planet and that we are directly affected by this activity regardless of when it occurred (could there possibly be events in the future that affect us now that we still have to learn of?). It is to engage with the whole of our being for we are personally affected by this revelation and by what this pursuit of truth has uncovered.

This is an example of one of the truths that science is uncovering, larger truths about the cosmos, but our individual person too has its own sense of truth. In Thomas Berry's essays on Confucianism he writes how the supreme achievement of the Chinese is total authenticity as a human being whereby *"man is established in his identity with himself, in his relationship with the total human community, and beyond that in his identity with both the cosmic and divine orders"*3. By being authentic, the person then participates in the universal order of things. One of the signs of authenticity according to Confucianism, is spontaneity in thought, speech and act. So integrated is the person who has attained this that they do not need to think before they speak or act because their actions and thoughts come from the very same place and truth as the natural and cosmic order of life itself. They have entered completely and without boundary into the very creative dynamics of the Universe. The way of achieving this perfection of human nature, according to Confucianism, is cultivation of our interior or spiritual development. To be authentic requires courage and as Sagan says, the desire to pursue the truth no matter where it leads. In Confucianism as Berry tells us, this is as much a way of feeling as a way of knowing where knowledge is broadened from the locus of the brain to include the heart and the emotions, so that the heart becomes understanding and the brain compassionate. The authentic one suffers from no division between rationale and gut. They are both equally valuable and integrated modes of knowing the world.

To reach the true nature of one's being is not an easy task. It is about activating that unique quantum of energy I mentioned earlier to give full expression to who you are. However, often our choices and the consequences they may incur can prevent us from wanting to go where our truth lies. New knowledge may require that we change the viewpoint that we live from. It may also require that we change our belief systems and what we think. It certainly requires that we consistently engage with life and with our experiences and to have the courage to no longer act from things we know not to be true.

Into the Depths

One of my favourite writer's is Oscar Wilde, a man deeply sensitive to the beauty of life as well as bewitched by the intoxicating seduction of pleasure. Wilde's financial, literary and personal life was shattered when he was sentenced to two years in prison for gross indecency, at minimum a questionable judgement and at maximum a serious miscarriage of justice. While there he wrote a letter entitled De Profundis, which is Latin meaning 'From the Depths', to his former lover. The letter is an examination of his life and his experiences, while at the same time a search for meaning in his present suffering. It is in many ways the journey of his spiritual growth. In it Wilde writes:

> *When first I was put into prison some people advised me to try and forget who I was. It was ruinous advice. It is only by realising what I am that I have found comfort of any kind......To regret one's own experiences is to arrest one's own development. To deny one's own experiences is to put a lie into the lips of one's own life. It is no less than a denial of the soul[4].*

It took Wilde's personal fall and the betrayal of one he had loved for him to arrive at this knowledge. Prison and its harshness presented a view of reality that he had hitherto never experienced. All the props and distractions, the hedonistic indulgences were no more and he was left to confront life in his own person, his own behaviours and his own thoughts. In this piece of writing, we can see he did not shirk from this examination but as the title suggests went down into the very depths of his broken and humiliated self. And what he found there, in my view, remains a lesson for us still on how human nature can, through suffering, develop. His musings are not bitter nor does he seek to attribute blame for this sudden and drastic change in circumstance. Instead he talks about forgiveness, about his own failings and about the friendships that sustain him. He talks about the pleasure that is still available to him in the contemplation of the natural beauty of the world, a beauty that remains as much for him as for anyone. He was to die three years after his release, destitute in Paris. His bravery in confronting who he was and the part his own self had to play in his demise, a courageous act of beauty, a benevolent human gesture preserved in ink. Wilde ends his letter with:

> ...still, I am conscious now that behind all this beauty, satisfying though it may be, there is some spirit hidden of which the painted forms and shapes are but modes of manifestation, and it is with this spirit that I desire to become in harmony……..society as we have constituted it, will have no place for me, has none to offer; but nature, whose sweet rains fall on unjust and just alike, will have clefts in the rocks where I may hide, and secret valleys in whose silence I may weep undisturbed.5

From 'De Profundis' we read of the learning of one who has suffered deeply and who looks within himself for the remedies to his own misery. Who can say whether this is the beginning of perfecting one's own human nature, but the unshrinking honesty with which Wilde levelled upon himself, his pursuit of the truth about his own life, his relationships, his values, his experiences was profound in its interiority and no doubt a painful exercise. Did he die reconciled and at peace? I don't know but I find in his letter a wisdom and authenticity that speaks of the deeper order of things, an authenticity that even though brought about by the hostile, condemnatory acts of people, remains sympathetic and compassionate towards humanity.

From Transcendence to Inscendence

For most of us, we will probably not face a prison sentence and such a drastic call of re-examination but there are always happenings that call us to deeper reflection and from that the ability to live a more authentic life. For my own self, I lived for a long time believing there to be a dichotomy between the spiritual reality and the physical reality. I thought that the physical life was a distraction from the real purpose of existence which was spiritual. I believed that the spirit could only be found in deep, deep silence in front of the altar of the church or by closing my eyes on this world and through prayer seeking to transcend it. This is what lead me into the convent, equal amounts spiritual thirst, equal amounts conviction that there had to be more to life than what I was living now. I wanted validation of my life, I wanted to feel like I was worth something and that my life and all I was, was not a meaningless accident.

I often think about this possibility, the possibility of meaningless. It stares me in the face like a vacuum daring me to take the jump, to be brave enough and see what happens. That it may all be a random coincidence and nothing more than a series of necessary adaptations and luck is a challenging and threatening thought, and one maybe we should all consider at least once in our lifetime; the fact that it may mean nothing at all. All our dreams and hopes, our love, our kind acts, may all mean nothing, an empty sheet blown by an arbitrary wind with nothing behind it only more emptiness. The freedom of this thought is inviting. It is also bleak and hollow. And yet the truth is that nobody who is living now can say with any empirical evidence and so with any certainty whether life means something or not. It is a choice we make. We choose to believe that there is more or we choose not to.

I made the choice when I entered the convent to believe there was more, and to worship this more, to dedicate my life to it. I lived with people who taught me about humility and sacrifice, whose day began and ended with prayer. People whom I wish I had the character to be like. Kind people. Considerate people. Disciplined and prayerful people. But I knew shortly after entering that I could not express myself fully there. I felt constrained and did not know what to think about for those periods I was meant to be praying. My mind wandered just like the planets. It flitted back and forth and could not climb over or calm the force of life or energy or whatever it is that infuses us. Maybe I was too undisciplined. My prayers were never finished. I wanted with my whole heart to be able to pray, to be fully present to the presence of God as I beseeched and praised him with words written hundreds and hundreds of years ago, but somehow I could never fully connect.

Much later after I had left the convent, I would pick up another essay of Thomas Berry's called 'The Dream of the Earth'. In it he writes one line that struck me powerfully. He says *"what is needed is not transcendence but 'inscendence', not the brain but the gene"*6. I was familiar with the term transcendence and knew it to mean our capacity to go beyond the limitations inherent in matter. Life advances by moving beyond these perceived limitations and evolving new ways of being. This is primarily how a time-developmental Universe works. When we transcend we go beyond our experience into the realm of what is both there and not there yet. It is a bridge between the physical and the spiritual, the way in which they connect. It is the indication of possibilities and one of the ways we discover and learn about our capabilities. But for the human at least, our desire and ability to transcend, innate or otherwise, has often blinded us to the sacredness that is inherent in the present. The idea of a transcendent God who is greater and other to this world, as well as Plato's Forms, had made me heedless to the divinity that permeates the Earth and forgetful of the fact that the Universe is the primary revelation of Divine mystery, even before scripture and even before prophet.

While this information about the effects of transcendence was new and informative, it was the concept of 'Inscendence' that really struck me. If transcendence is what takes us beyond then inscendence must be what takes us 'in'. If transcendence takes us out of the physical world, then inscendence takes us back into the physical world. I had left the convent by this stage knowing that I could not stay there and remain true to myself. At the time I could not articulate why but reading this sentence clarified the decision I had made. I didn't have it in me to transcend the world, I needed to be part of it. This was where I found and related to the divine. Through my senses and all the ways that the world became alive to me.

I don't think in all my breathing days that I will ever surpass the feeling of being submersed in the salty, cradling ocean on a hot summer's day. It slows me down, empties my mind and makes me feel alive at the same time, no monkey mind or jumping thoughts just an overwhelming sense of gratitude and an amazement that such a simple act of life can produce such an overwhelming sense of wellbeing. I feel it as gift. As sheer joy. As a taste of the sacred. I feel it as one of the most direct experiences and communion with the Divine. And then I watch the young children squealing in delight as they are bashed by the waves they are trying to jump over and think how could there be a more true prayer than the moment when we delight and revel in the creation, transcending daily drudgery not by closing our eyes on the world but by total participation in it?

There are other ways too that we try to live an authentic life, a life that is whole. This is by ensuring that our thoughts are reflective of our experience. If how we view the world does not match our experience of the world, then we must have the courage to change how we think. Similarly if our knowledge of the world does not match our actions, then we must change our actions or seek more knowledge. There must be an integrity, a seamless relation between what we say we do and what we do, between what we believe and how we act. Authenticity begins with integrity and integrity begins with singleness of being, where there is no discrepancy between belief, thought and action but rather they interdependently continue to evolve and to change as our experience and knowledge informs them.

The Night Sky that is Past

To look into the night sky is to watch what has already taken place. Such a strange fact to grapple with. The past so visible here in the present. What kind of a Universe can do that, blur the lines between time, make light travel and use the past to illuminate the sky of the present? Even the very concept of light travelling itself, a ridiculing affront to our once held believe in a fixed, unchanging Universe. And yet someone, many people, had to uncover this fact. They had to be brave enough to follow where the consequences of this knowledge would take them, like Copernicus and Galileo after him. Were they perfecting their own human nature or helping us to perfect ours? Their knowledge and where it lead them bringing humanity into a deeper understanding of this Universe. Their knowledge and their integrity towards it ensuring that they themselves began to participate in the dynamics of life, making people aware, helping them to describe this world, making us question our assumptions and changing how we live. It is authenticity according to Confucius that enables this participation in the cosmic order, authenticity that enables the cosmos to work through our very own being. Being true, perhaps this then is one of the greatest acts that we can gift back to the world?

Chapter 11
Suffering

There is an ache at the centre of humanity. Nietzsche once said *"To live is to suffer, to survive is to find some meaning in the suffering"*. There is so little explanation offered to us in the way of the world. We have had to craft our own, we have become meaning makers, part of this world and at the same time observing it. We know enough to know that there is a longing that runs through life but we do not know if that longing resides in only us or if it is part of this beautiful world too and simply passes through us?

We fall in love, make our dreams and try to create a life, only to find that it is not how we had desired or even as we had imagined. What is the point of dreams if they cannot be fulfilled or of love if it cannot be returned or of life if it is a struggle to rise from the bed and be present in the day just until you can sleep again? All the sharp, bitter aspects of this existence that make it heavy and joyless and dry, and then us, shackled to the Earth with our little human minds, flailing and exasperated and hopelessly trying to make sense of it all. Dreams and love and life – what is the point?

I once met a girl sitting outside at a bus station. She was thin, skinny even. The bones in her knees stuck out like a small child's and her hands trembled. Her clothes were dirty and worn and her hair was stuck to her head, slick with grease. Her face had patches of brown make-up but I could still see the red marks of her ravaged youth showing on her cheeks. Her eyes were glazed and bloodshot. Her daughter, a toddler, was dressed in pyjamas and a coat that must have once been white but now was dirty and grey. She struck up conversation with me, asked me for a cigarette and told me about her hangover as she began to open a can of beer and drink from it. I thought she felt embarrassed. It was only 11.30am.

It seemed to me that in her one, brief existence all those bitter aspects of life had converged. At some point she must have made a choice, maybe flippantly carried away by excitement or maybe with reluctance, but this choice was bearing down on her now, burying her so deep that her body seemed unoccupied, a dead space behind her eyes. I thought of her for my whole journey home. Where does the spirit go at times like that? How could she be so vacant, so empty? I thought of all that I was learning about the development of the cosmos and the resilient nature of life and tried to fit the two together; what I had just seen and this new knowledge of the Universe that no longer seemed connected. What was her story, the role that she played? Billions of years of creation, rolling through time and formation and manifestation, each a once-off, never to be repeated, so uniquely precious and divinely inhabited and then her, lost. I thought that if I could talk to her that I could reach her, but then hesitated until the moment was lost. What are words? Who am I to say them?

What would it mean to her to be told that she was conceived in a star, present at the Big Bang and waiting for the time when life could bring her forth? What would it feel like to her when people tell her that, open their mouths and talk at her, the words falling off their tongue, sentences clogging her ears, trying to find space amongst the desperate thoughts that already fill her head, buzzing, whirring and exhausting. How can it matter as she claws through the day and its hazy happenings, her body pleading for drink, shaking in its insidious desire and her full, frenzied mind struggling to evacuate one clear thought? What was life revealing to her, what was life revealing through her? What dreamed inside her and where had these dreams brought her? Surely no-one can be born just to be an example to others? I thought about the other ways that suffering passes through the world, about Syria and the carnage there, so unnecessary, so violent. Or the famine in Somalia and its resultant refugee camps with conditions that reminded me of those paintings of hell. War, famine, drugs but it doesn't have to be so drastic or so extreme; it filters down in some way and in some form to everybody, a broken heart, a death, a betrayal. Pain just seems so easy to create.

I thought too of how suffering nearly always comes from loss and how loss does not exclude anyone. From birth we can even measure life through loss – the loss of innocence, the loss of trust, the loss of hope, the loss of youth as if from the moment we arrive on this planet things get progressively worse, as if we are born whole and full and the rest of our life is coming to terms with the fact that our life is a lesson in diminishment. I tried to reconcile the extensive nature of loss with the abundant generosity of life. It jarred.

But it's not only our losses, it's our human intention too, the cruelty in our remarks, the malicious intent of our words, the callousness of our actions bringing more pain into the world, passing it on. It's the way in which we nurture our hurts, feed them, afraid to let them go, remembering them, calling on them, using them against others. Why do we do that?

Pains of the body and pains of the spirit. What a fragile species. I wondered where did the pain start with that girl. I could see it in her body, but doesn't pain of that depth come from the spirit? Doesn't it work from inside out, from the place that is hidden to our senses, that seems inaccessible to us until it shapes our desires, the place that creates our dreams and our hopes and claims our loves – is this not the spirit? But how could we hurt in our spirit, in this our purest of parts, and what is the pain that is born from there? Is it the acknowledgement of all our failures, the collision of our aspirations with our limitations and the hard and empty, hollow sound that collision makes? How could she be so hopeless? Dreams, love, life and loss. There had to be a connection.

Life

Who is to say what is a life well spent or what is a life worth having? Our time is so brief here, like the flame of a candle bursting forth when first ignited and getting progressively smaller and more tentative with each sudden movement and impact until it is finally snuffed out. We hurtle along through school, marriage, children, house, car, job and all the other indicators we have for a successful life and then realise we never really knew what we were trying to achieve in the first place. How could we? In comparison to the others, we are so young. Even the flowers. The aven catches my eye as it sits wind-swept in the pockets of the rock, her white and yellow a statement about the simple beauty and resilience of life that makes me wonder about my own excessively analytical nature and inability to just be present in the moment. She is a creature among others letting the world look after her. Why does life involve thought? Why do I involve thought?

Sometimes it doesn't feel like the world is real to me or that I am real in the world. The distance in my head makes it feel like I am living in spite of myself. A life given to me without my asking. From where and for what? Suddenly we are here, young and eager with all this time stretching out before us waiting to be lived. We tangle ourselves in knots wanting to use it properly, not knowing what to do or how to fill it, what our life should be. How did it get so difficult just to be alive? The swallow glides through the sky on a spring evening, returning after her epic journey over ocean and desert right to the very spot she left a year ago and I envy her certainty, her fixed sense of purpose. But for us, the human, there is always something to question the worth of our existence. Not enough money, not enough food, not enough love, an addiction, a childhood abuse, the gaping emptiness of the mind that struggles to feel real, the loneliness of the heart that struggles to feel alive.

And life is lived in the mind as much as in the body. Strange how we can disappear beneath the layers of our wandering thoughts and self-seeking analysis, fall into the trap of thinking that it is our own head that sorts it out and ignore the fresh feel of a summer breeze on our clamy skin as it cools us effortlessly. At the same time trying to grasp the fact that others are walking around with their head as full of thoughts as our own, each person a microcosm of the whole of creation trying to make sense of their lives. And we can't see their thoughts or touch them or read them – an entire world holed up in the head of each person only to be revealed as they wish.

That girl in the bus station, I wondered had she stopped trying to understand her life, given up when events no longer seemed rational to her. Simply stopped trying to figure it out and began to quieten the destructiveness of her thought by opting out.

Our journey through life and the thoughts that understand it are so deeply interwoven. The thoughts that interpret what happens to us, that make us sad for all that could have been but never was, that turn young smiles into bitterness, and hope into cynicism, that justify opportunism over generosity, and make us feel defeated, wondering how we could ever have been hopeful or had expectations in the first place. Or our thoughts that make us feel grateful when there is little left, that make us feel love when we are alone, that fill our heads with the boundless possibilities contained in each new day.

Dreams

And the days pass so quickly, free wheeling from one event of our lives to the next and missing the hundred little joys of simple being that happens in between them; making plans, changing them, reacting and adapting, human spokes in a wheel relentlessly spinning until eventually staying upright becomes the hardest part and the luxury of dreaming becomes resigned to an indulgent comfort that reminds us of what it was like to be young. Mostly our dreams die with us, never having had the chance or circumstances to take flight; they lie locked into our coffins, unfulfilled and dead. Dreams and suffering, it seems so obvious how one could lead to the other. Our dreaming human species saturating the world with thoughts and desires, seven billion people, seven billion aspirations, seven billion dreams and one planet to hold them all – how could there possibly be room for everybody's?

I thought again of the friends I had made in the Philippines, those that had no electricity or running water and whose houses were a combination of iron sheeting and wood with the direct and unadorned Earth as their floor. They did not have sitting-rooms or bathrooms or utilities. They did not have cars or bicycles or scooters. Were they worse off than us? I never thought so. After staying there though I wondered about the dreams of the people who lived there, if they were the same as my own or if they dreamed of more practical things like running water, electric lights, concrete houses. Did they dream of travelling the world, of 'careers', of the strange concept of self-actualisation? Or were their dreams larger, fed by the heartbeat of life which continued to pulse through their village, the Earth there unsuppressed as yet by the incessant drone of industrialisation.

I wondered what a dream was and where it comes from and if choice had a role to play in the dreams that emerge from us. Just like pain, I wondered if there were dreams of the spirit and dreams of the flesh, dreams of material comfort and dreams of spiritual peace and if the attainment of one affected the other? So quietly they are born in us, slipping into our consciousness when we think we have the world blocked out, awakening us to the possibilities beyond our mind's horizon, stretching and alluring us. Our body may have limits but our mind does not. It is free to go beyond what we have ever experienced, to picture ourselves in places where we have never been and with people we do not know, in circumstances we desire. Isn't that what a dream is, a desire. Desiring our dreams and dreaming our desires. This curious human ability that has led some to shape civilisations and broken so many, many others.

I thought again of that girl at the bus station who had come for me to symbolise the effect of suffering. She must also, at one time, have had dreams which had filled her head and heart and brightened her young eyes, lying down with her at night and accompanying her through the day, the soft padding of hope which drove her actions. Until something took them. Maybe she had learned what I was only beginning to and what those people in that village had always known, that life was not about her or her dreams but about something much greater than any one human desire could encompass and any one species could transmit. And that was it, so simple, and at the same time, so ironic a consequence of being human, the connection between dreams and suffering.

For what does one do with the knowledge that I am not special but as unexceptional and ordinary as all those billions of others who walked the Earth before me and who walk the Earth with me now, who tried to shape the world to fit them and whose names and lives and deeds have faded out of existence just as surely as mine will?

The world does not fit us, does not bend to our desire but holds steadfast to its own and we are left with our limited understanding and our limited intellect to crumble beneath the realisation of our own insignificance. The disappointment mingles with disbelief, disappointment that eventually hardens into bitterness and bitterness which rages and laments at the human condition and sours the goodness of life. A broken dream, some aspiration that was never reached, all that I could have been lost in who I have become, all that my one shot at life could have been contained in this meaningless existence that never really got started. No wonder life is so hard – how are we ever to catch up with who we think we should be?

And this was it, one of the reasons we suffer - our heightened human sense of self, the expectation and sense of entitlement that we carry around and impose upon the world just because we are alive and we are human. The delusional dreams we concoct in our wonder world of plastic and synthetics where people don't get old or defecate and there are no human limits, where the Earth is there for our taking. In this bubble box of our own making, how could there be anything but suffering?

Chapter 12
Perhaps another Dream?

But this is not the totality of the world or the totality of life, this suffering, loss, poverty, pain and our empty, foolish dreams. This is just part of it and often how we just feel it to be. Suffering is pervasive and we play our part in exercising it, but there is more, so much more. There is the sky and the rains, the sea and the winds, the trees and the sweet, scented flowers, the swooping, diving, singing birds, the gentle, spotted ladybird, the prowling cat. The world is abundant and full. And it is for everyone. And all we need is contained right where we are, in this abundance, and it is enough. And it, and we, are never diminished but rather we grow and expand and complexify, just as this one single, seamless enterprise that is the Universe does.

It seems to me that a lot of suffering stems from loss and that loss has to do with how we see ourselves in the world and what we think we are here for. If we think that we are separate to the world, arbitrary and accidental, then everything is loss because life only happens in and through our own existence, making everything else superfluous and containing no meaning in and for itself. This is what makes a death final because the person who has died is gone, as is our experience of them. If we see ourselves as being here to enhance our own lives only, whether through accumulation or education or career, even location, then, again, anything that we perceive to be a diminishment of these criteria will be taken as a loss and as a result create some form of suffering.

But our worth does not come from externalities. Our worth comes from the fact that we are here and because we are here, we participate. If we see ourselves as brought forth by life, bound into life, and participating in life, then loss takes on another dimension, in that what might be seen as loss can now be understood as change. Because nothing is ever lost. It is held inside us, defining us, becoming us, in our memories, in our heart, in our thoughts, in our being. How could anything be lost when all that ever was is in us and when we remain in all that will ever be and connected to all beings? Isn't that what evolution is? Held by the spirit that has breathed us into existence so that we can never be taken out again, with our birth we take our place amongst all else that has ever lived, never to be extinguished and never to be replaced. Bound so totally into the web of life that a death, even our own death, or a broken heart or a crushed dream although hitting into the very gut of us, will never be enough to diminish us.

It also seemed to me that a lot of suffering stemmed from what we think life is for and the dreams that we grow because of this - our dreams of wealth, our dreams of possession and power and fame, our dreams of success, even our dreams of stability and security.

But what of the dream that creates gases and dust until these create stars which in turn create galaxies – what is that dream? What is the dream that creates a sun, and from the debris of a dead and disseminated star, a solar system? What is the dream that creates Earth, a planet teeming with life, life in the water, life in the trees, life in the soil; a planet bursting with a variety of expressions of being, beings that fly, beings that swim, beings that sing and dance and play and think, beings who then themselves dream. What is the dream that creates the being who knows that they are part of this dream and aims to understand it? What is the dream that creates forgiveness and hope and love?

There is another dream, a dream that is larger than ours, physically begun some 14 billion years ago. This is the dream of the spirit. Through time, as we have learned, this dream is becoming slowly manifest, revealing a magnificence and beauty and brilliance that we can only stand in awe of. This is the dream that has brought life in all its myriad of diverse formations; this is the dream that brings thought; that brings us.

And we suffer because we don't pay attention to this dream or seek to hear it speak but rather let it be drowned by noises and events and ideas that only serve humanity, noises and events that ignore that dream and follow our own dreams under the illusion that we have individual successes and that there is such a thing as individual advancement. To know this greater dream we must go deeper than our own desire. And this is always happening to us if we only have eyes to see.

The beauty of a tender moment that softens us and makes us peaceful, dipping into the knowledge that we have forgotten but that is ours, giving us a glimpse of the eternity of things, the benevolence that flows through life, and the gentle kindness at the heart of breath. The penetrating gaze of a newborn child that looks straight through us as if it knows all that we have ever done; the brief, wordless touch of an elder to a youth that carries away disappointment and once again infuses enthusiasm. This dream of love, of compassion, of unity, is the dream that flows through life, connecting us all and holding us all together, alluring and enticing us.

But even if we change how we see the world and our place in it, there will still be suffering. Even if we begin to know and learn our story, our story that is 13.8 billion years old, there will still be a longing at the heart of humanity, an ache and a restlessness that always leaves us wishing and wanting more, so that we are never totally fulfilled. But as the cosmos develops, so too do we. As life evolves, so too do we. Could it be that as a species, we are developing, so that the pain we feel now is just the pain of one who is still a child and who has not yet become who we are supposed to be? Is it because the Universe is not finished with us and at some level we know this and ache to be more that we do not feel fulfilled? Is it because the Universe is still growing us that we do not feel complete? Could it also be that the way that it grows us is through suffering?

The arrival of humanity has added a new depth of experience to the Universe. We have the capacity to feel so deeply; to feel love and hope, to feel the pain of another. We have the capacity for forgiveness. We also have the capacity for thought. But we do not often choose these capacities over others. The society we have built for ourselves, a society which is itself also evolving, has programmed us towards prioritising other capacities, such as achievement, individualism, competition. These access other parts of our nature. It is only when we are jolted from the physical and material allurement of life that we come to know the deeper side of our nature, the side that is spirit. It is only when we are in touch with this deeper side that we fully realise and begin to see how deeply connected and related we are to every other single being. It is our relationship with the spirit that determines how we live and who we become. Thomas Berry once said that matter is nothing without form, and what is form only spirit. The way in which we shape our lives is the way in which we express our spirit.

So I ask again, what is the point of our dreams if they cannot be fulfilled or of love if it cannot be returned or of life if it is persistently a struggle? The point is this, with each denial or dashed hope, we experience something divine, we experience the power of this dream of the spirit showing us that life has a larger trajectory than my own desire. We feel in suffering the timeless quality that touches the very essence of who we are. Grief empties us, de-robes us of the daily concerns of life. It erases the layers of understanding and explanation that we have built over the years and that make us comfortable and assured, almost apathetic, quelling our curiosity, until its mighty hand once again throws us into the incomprehensible mystery that is life. With each denial is the realisation that life is not about 'me', and the chance to give ourselves over to what it may be about, the chance to learn and reconnect to this dream of the spirit. These experiences bring us deeper into that mystery, activating dimensions of our being that previously slept, showing the depths that we contain within us and the meaning that permeates life.

Chapter 13
The Meaning of Life to Earth

Maybe it is arrogant to speak about a greater dream than the human dream, more arrogant still to think that one can understand the spirit, and yet, the more I learn of this Universe, the more it seems that there is some larger scheme afoot. As an illustration of this, one need only to focus on Earth and how it has developed since its formation 4 billion years ago. This point is inadvertently addressed in the book 'The New Universe and the Human Future' by Nancy Abrams and Joel Primack, when they ask the question of what is the meaning of life to Earth. The question struck me because it reverses the contemporary way of thinking which is what is the meaning of *my* life and why am *I* here, and instead focuses on life as a singular enterprise of Earth and asks how does life serve Earth and what does it mean for Earth to have life. From this perspective, we can see just how much life has added to Earth, how much more detailed and elaborate Earth has become because of life. The changes Earth has undergone are indicative of an adventure that is far, far greater than the human, an adventure begun long before the human even emerged. But could it also be argued, that they are indicative too, of a dream that is far more imaginative and far more creative than any dream the human could possibly aspire to? Let us look at what might be the meaning of life to Earth but before we can do that, we need to first ask what it is we mean by 'life' and revisit how it has evolved and transformed.

Definitions of Life

Life by its nature is difficult to define. Biologists have a list of characteristics which they attribute to it. These are: heritable reproduction (heritable means that offspring resemble their parents); the ability to undergo evolution by natural selection; metabolism (using energy to move or grow); growth and development; movement; response to stimuli; adaptation and ordered structure. Most biologists generally agree on the first two characteristics, sometimes the first three but then others are less firm about what characterises life. Some scientists say that the entire Universe is living and that life itself is a property of the Universe because all the elements needed as the building blocks for life were formed in the stars and in the big bang. Richard Fortey writes "*life is not just a matter of chemistry: it is a cooperation between molecules to produce a consequence infinitely greater than the sum of its parts.*"[1] Physicist Larry Edwards says how life is a community behaviour, a capacity of this Earth which bestows an intimacy on the planet as each species and their function serve to shape the other species they interact with.

These definitions illustrate the elusive nature of life and how efforts to define it are consistently vague and unsatisfactory. Not only do they fail to produce an explanation or definition of what life is but they also only deal with the physical aspects of it. They do not deal with the psychic or spiritual aspects of life such as consciousness or the mind or equally important, its origin.

Origins of Life

The question of how life began has eluded some of the greatest thinkers this planet has known. Richard Dawkins writes "*the origin of life [is] the origin of true heredity......[it was] not a probable event, but it only had to happen once*". Darwin himself wrote "*It is mere rubbish thinking at present of the origin of life; one might as well think of the origin of matter*"[2]. But why shouldn't the origin of life or the origin of matter concern us. Is that not *the* question? Doesn't the answer or even how we think about this have huge implications for how we see the world and how we see ourselves and our place in the world? Teilhard de

Chardin writes how "*the beginnings of all things tend to become materially imperceptible to us*"3, that is, we can never truly know the beginnings or the origins of anything. There are theories and hypotheses about the origins of life among them the RNA World hypothesis but until now, with the current consensus of science, we can say that life had its beginnings in mystery.

Why should this matter? What is the significance of not knowing the beginning of something? It is significant because it illustrates the nebulous and unquantifiable but equally valid aspect of reality, this cloud of unknowing from which life springs. There is something at our root that remains beyond human comprehension and scientific explanation, something perhaps not fully manifest in the physical world. The Universe began as the size of a pinprick, minute on any level of measurement and then expanded and grew into galaxies, stars, planets, people, animals, birds, flowers – the list is endless. The potential for all that ever was and is contained in this initial dense and compact quantum of energy. From this there has gradually been an unfolding of beings, a manifestation of whatever the Big Bang was, a manifestation that through time is becoming increasingly more complex both in form and structure.

Could we go further with this point as Jean Gebser did in The Ever-present Origin and say that this 'beginning' although as of yet, unknown, seeks in fact to be known and understood and with the passage of time becomes ever more transparent? Who would have thought three hundred years ago that we would have learned of the basic components of matter or that we would be able to describe the early Earth or trace our human lineage all the way back to its birthplace in Africa? Who would have thought sixty years ago that we would have left our planet, travelled to space and taken a photograph of Earth? Who would have thought fifteen years ago that scientists would be recreating the Big Bang in a science laboratory in Geneva with extraordinary results?

This mystery of origins is also remarkable because it is indicative of how the world comes to us – not always rationally or scientifically but suddenly and mysteriously and out of that mystery grows something that the human being describes but also out of that mystery that the human being describes, grows the human being. The world is not all hard edges, cut and dried, waiting to be observed and analysed and labelled. It is equally a world of thought and emotion, of dreams and intuition - the invisible nature of its being permeates its existence. And it is this intangible, spiritual or psychic quality which begins to be revealed as we learn more about its physical aspects. Language for instance, spoken language in particular, through which we transcend the limits of our body and engage in a communion that is beyond the physical, a communion based on symbol and concept and from which we construct our reality and through which we articulate and explain our reality.

It is important to note that the physical and the psychic, the tangible and the spiritual are not separate as is often emphasized but rather two aspects of one reality and it is in the combination of these, form and spirit, psyche and physical that we have life, its origins a mystery, contained in a deeper realm of knowing than is available to us at present but its evolution a mesmerising description of ever increasing complexity and ever increasing diversity.

Evolution of Life

Although it cannot explain or describe its origins, there are some things however that science can tell us had to happen in order for life to originate. We are in what is known as the habitable zone i.e. our planet is exactly the right distance from the sun. Not only that but the balance between the size of Earth and the internal fires at the centre of the planet also had to be exactly right – a larger planet would never have achieved the surface temperatures for life to arrive and a smaller planet would have burned out. This tells us that although life on our planet was not a given that it was probable and that it would have happened on some bio-physical planet in some place at some time in the Universe. Brian Swimme surmises that the Universe was preparing for it; I like to say that there is a curious precision to this mystery.

Obscurely coming into existence around 3.8 billion years ago, life emerged in a relatively simple form as the prokaryotic cell of whom every creature is a descendant. A billion years later there emerged the eukaryotic cell with its nucleus and chromosome and ability to sexually reproduce. The ability to reproduce contained the capacity of memory and the capacity to pass on information; to prioritise what works and should be preserved such as the chlorophyll molecule and the creation of photosynthesis and respiration, the eye of the Trilobyte – all these essential components for the existence and form of life to take shape as we know it today.

Over 3 billion years, life changed in form and structure, transformed and diversified into plant and animal and fish and insect and reptile and mammal. All life being born in the sea and then later, mysteriously and curiously driven, emerging from it. Some one hundred million years ago with a beauty all their own, flowers appeared and then sixty million years ago birds took to the sky and mammals roamed the woods. From the shell to the vertebrate to the first jawed fish, the first lungs, the first wings, the first eye, endless, endless firsts and endless, endless diversification.

From physics comes chemistry and from chemistry comes biology and from biology, life. It is a seamless event. Duncan writes *"There seems to be a general trend in the universe toward assembling structures of increasing complexity out of simpler building block"*4. In their book, The New Universe and the Human Future Abrams and Primack write:

> *...that's exactly what evolution means: whatever simple materials are given to time as resources, even just particles and energy, time will use, and complexity, possibly in the form of life and even moral life, will*

emerge. *'From so simple a beginning'* Darwin wrote,
*'endless forms most beautiful and most wonderful have
been, are being, evolved* 5.

The human has also gone through its own forms of
evolution from Homo habilis who created the first tools to Homo
erectus who discovered fire to Homo sapiens – the one who knows
they know, the self-reflective creature of Earth. Our evolution
however continues, but this time we have a larger role to play in
its direction. While the Earth has evolved over billions of years in
a self-regulating and self-organising manner, with the arrival of
the human being these natural forces began to be manipulated.
Although one of the youngest species, the consciousness of the
human, the way in which we think, has the ability to alter the
planet. We can witness this in the removal of forest, the building
of roads and railway tracks; the preservation of wetlands, the
creation of cities, the pollution of lakes and rivers. It is through
this ability, this ability to reflect, to think, to be conscious that we
are now able to know the story that science describes to us of the
evolution of life and the evolution of Earth. It is also this ability
which will inform how we will act and what kind of a species we
will become, how we will view life. It is no small gift but rather
the manifestation of life into thought, the next step of the
evolution. A new dimension, a thinking planet exercised
powerfully through, although not uniquely through, the human
mind. It is because of this that we need to know where we have
come from and what has come before us. We need to know our
story, this story of the Universe and the part we play, the part that
we could play.

What is the meaning of life to Earth?

Following this brief and highly unsatisfactory recount of
the origins of life and its evolution, we can now ask what would
Earth be like without life. What has life brought to Earth? It is near
impossible to imagine our planet without birds in the sky, without

children and trees and flowers, without butterflies. These are the beautiful images and indeed, there has been with the arrival of life a fundamental beauty created by this planet. But life has brought more than beauty or perhaps it is because of what it has brought, that it is beautiful.

Seen from space our Earth was remarkable not only for its quality as one living and inter-related organism but also for its colour – a shimmering globe of blue and green and white. Astronaut, Edgar Mitchell when seeing Earth from space said:

> *...suddenly, from behind the rim of the Moon, in long, slow-motion moments of immense majesty, there emerges a sparkling blue and white jewel, a light delicate sky-blue sphere laced with slowly swirling veils of white, rising gradually like a small pearl in a thick sea of black mystery. It takes more than a moment to fully realise this is Earth....home 6.*

Life has brought colour and in this colour, there is beauty. Who has not been hit by the yellow of the daffodil bursting forth from its green stalk, announcing its arrival after the dark journey of winter? Or by the Kingfisher soaring by, an arrow of royal blue and then suddenly the flash of red from its breast or the unblemished white of the swan, tipped with its orange beak sitting on the muddy waters of the canal. Life brings colour, a beautiful carefree splurge of differentiated vibrancy.

Life also brings music and in music, again there is beauty, not only in the music of Beethoven and Bach, but in the music of the birds, the music of the seas and the wind, the music of the trees, the music of the human voice. There is beauty in the music of the city, bustling and beeping and noisy, in the music of the countryside, of lambs bleating and the long sonorous sighs of cattle. There is beauty too in the smells that life has brought, the sweet freshness of a new born baby's head, lilies at Easter, roses in summer, coffee in the morning. There is beauty in the dramatic and endless forms of life, the shape of a horse as it gallops and extends its body, or a dolphin breaching the waves, the majestic ruggedness of a mountain, and the intricacy of a seahorse. Life has brought a beauty to Earth, a beauty expressed through colour, smell and form, a beauty that arouses the senses, fills the mind and evokes the imagination, a beauty expressed in countless different ways.

We can also say that with life, the Earth began to speak and hear and look, began to experience herself. With the mouth came taste, with the nose, scent, with the eyes vision. And so with life, Earth began to experience and notice herself, to taste her fruits and smell her flowers, to watch her storms and bathe in her sunsets.

Through the combination of the senses came admiration and communication. We could begin to talk, not only of Earth's, but of the Universe's wonders, her majesty, her mystery, her terrors. We wrote songs and poetry in celebration and awe. We began to observe the colour of the peacock's tail, to identify the voice of the lark, fear the prowl of the black bear. Through the capacity of the senses we began to admire and to learn from each other, share experience, and so deepen and internalise relationships, each sense adding to a creature's ability to revel in this planet and its sounds and colours, thus each creature providing the space and form for the Earth to feel and to deepen, providing the space for the Earth to love. Life has, through depth of feeling, brought increased interiority.

It is difficult to write of life and what it brings to Earth in a purely rational way. It is more than the brain, it is the whole, the heart, the spirit, the body, complete, and it moves the human being at every level. There is a mystery to it, not only in its origins, but in how it continues, in how it evolves. This mystery has forged a curiosity and a wonder in the heart of humanity who seeks to know and understand it, who seeks to reveal it, and we do this with the consciousness that life has also brought. It is this consciousness which confers, in quite a literal sense, 'meaning' to Earth. Without consciousness such questions as 'what is the meaning of life to Earth?' would never arise, they would never exist. Through our consciousness we create stories about our existence, we give meaning to being here. This differs among people but it is a universal phenomenon that the human being needs to create meaning. With science and technology we have been able to penetrate into the workings of nature, to unfold some of its secrets, to build up a picture of what Earth and this Universe are like. We are, in a very real sense, the Universe, through Earth, exploring and understanding herself, revealing herself on a deeper level than was previously possible. Before consciousness, the Earth evolved "on remote control", now, we not only evolve but we seek to explain and describe and give meaning to this evolution. Life has evolved into such a position that it has begun to explain itself. Life has brought thought and with it, description and explanation.

The darker side of this evolutionary achievement of consciousness is that we can now manipulate evolutionary processes. We can choose how we will move forward and how we will evolve. If we decide that as a species, life will be better when each person has a four wheel drive, we will use the Earth in such a way as to produce these vehicles to the detriment of the planet and its ecosystems as well as to our bodies. If we decide that virtual communication is more effective than face to face communication, we will prioritise and develop our computer skills to the detriment of conversation and shared social experiences. If we decide that money and the accumulation of possessions is the only way to make us happy, we will deny ourselves the experience of intimacy and trust that is gained from living in simplicity and integrity within the natural order.

Every decision is a contribution towards the future and every decision has a consequence. With all the positives that life has brought to Earth – beauty, colour, speech, thought, feeling, love - where will we bring it now? Life has through time, through evolution and through the consciousness of humanity become its own evolutionary driving force, determining the future of Earth.

Are we wise enough to hold this position? Do we recognise the responsibility of this? How we progress will be the ultimate meaning of life to Earth.

Chapter 14
Is this the Human Role?

We are very new arrivals in the cosmos, a struggling, bewildered species, trying to understand ourselves and our existence; trying to find meaning in our lives. Our history is deep, much deeper than we previously thought. Our lives are connected, much more connected than we previously knew. This new information from science about the Universe does not give us answers but it does give us clues, clues to what we could be, clues as to how we should relate and how we should act, what we need. And so after we have learned our history and felt the pull of this other dream, after we have come to know our capacity to love, stood beneath its endless flow of hope and promise, its stilling warmth; after we have held the gift of consciousness and all the knowledge and learning we have harnessed through it, entered into its depths, our own depths and are silent at what is revealed to us there; after we have realised that we do not come as one shining piece of light but as light and darkness, a being of paradox and ambiguity, as one who is limited but can aspire beyond their limits, as one who is immortal but also must die; and after we realise that the Universe is soaked in the Divine, each creature and plant and tree an expression of the sacred, telling another story of divinity, of her diversity, her complexity, her depth, perhaps then we might come to know why we were brought forth.

Personalization

I know that it is not for one person to write about what is the place of the human being. It is not for one person to stand outside her species, presently numbering 7 billion, and to say what this species is on Earth for and what its contribution to life, to this planet and to the Universe are. Each person can only offer insight and wisdom from their own experience, can only give an opinion, even though learned and studied and researched, an opinion nonetheless, which no matter how we try, always remains personal. And my opinion is that as we cannot escape our own personhood, as we can never exist separate from it, that perhaps this is the key - to become as personal and as integrated as we can in order that we may reflect the Universe, express it and experience it, admire it in our own unique way. In order that we may personalise it.

Teilhard wrote about "the personalizing Universe". He wrote that it is the task of each of us "*to establish in ourselves an absolutely original centre where the Universe is reflected in a unique and inimitable way: precisely our self, our personality*"1. In a Universe that thrives on diversity and differentiation, we must not be afraid of what makes us different but seek to deepen it. And eventually when we are comfortable and familiar in the realisation that we do not think the same, nor love the same, nor understand the same, then we must express that which is only of us, gift it back to the Universe from whence it came and add to the kaleidoscope and tapestry that life is. Add the deepest awareness and expression of our own self - a life lived from its depths.

Rilke in Letters to a Young Poet writes "*Think, dear Sir, of the world which you carry within yourself, and call this thinking what you like; let it be memory of your own childhood or longing for your own future – only pay attention to what arises within you, and set it above everything you notice about you. Your inmost happening is worth your whole love.*2" He later says "*we shall also learn gradually to realize that it is out of mankind that what we call destiny proceeds, not into them from without* "3. Our development and authenticity as a person must come from the exploration of our own interior depths, from the deep solitude and silence wherein we can hear God speak and learn how we must speak, where the noises and voices that are constant in our mind are silenced until we arrive in the place beyond thought, beyond knowledge, beyond ourselves. In this place lies the same fabric that breathed the fireball into existence; that transformed hydrogen and helium into stars, and star dust into planets. The same essence that shines the moon and grows the sunflower, that forgives a failing and kisses a child. The same essence that is seeking to create again.

Too often, we speak of professionalism and efficiency. We pay homage to these concepts and seek to imbibe and reproduce them, make them our aim. But what is professionalism only the increased dehumanization of someone, where we sacrifice feelings of solidarity and compassion and unity in order to become the most efficient cog in the corporate machine. Our human role, is not to be professional but to be as human as we can, as fully human as we possibly can. Loving others, caring for others, serving others, being foolish and vulnerable and making as many mistakes in our short lives as we possibly can. Is there anything more human than to make a mistake? Doesn't the Universe itself as it unfolds it's mighty self, grope and chance and make mistake? Personalisation is to feel and to know my own centre, the centre that beats in me but also beats in every one else and to live and to love and to breath out of this centre knowing that there is no model for anybody's life, no instruction manual, no map or blueprint to follow only the seed that lies in the depths of us waiting to be discovered, waiting to bloom in us.

We cannot see the future, so we must listen to the past, listen as it guides us and coaxes us, as it is present in our cells and as it beats in our bones. We are new but many have lived before us, bringing life forward so that we may be, and now we take up the thread and begin to unfold our own part, a part that nobody else can play. Our destiny as a species is dependent on each person coming to know their own centre in order that they might contribute to the whole. And so we embrace the pain and the suffering for the lessons these must teach us, we embrace the joys and the hopes and the mystery that is our existence. We take them all gratefully and celebrate them and live them through as fully and as compassionately and as thoughtfully as we can. With every life adding a new dimension to joy and a new dimension to pain, deepening the feeling of the Universe, increasing its creativity, increasing its love, giving flesh to its spirit and completing the whole.

And we wonder, we wonder about our life and we wonder where we came from and we seek for answers.

Witness

The last sixty- five million years of Earth's history have been one of its most productive, a time of mesmerising creativity where the Earth flowered in bright and blazing colours, where the grasses spread their blanket of green and the forests rose stoic and serene. The Earth gave birth to the horse and the cow, the whale and the dolphin, the monkey and the elephant. She gave birth to the rosebush and the lilac tree and the jasmine vine perfuming the planet with their intoxicating scents until eventually with an imagination and a spirit shaped by the beauty of her creatures, the bounty of her fruits, and the majesty of her shape and colour, she gave birth to our species and through us her ability to admire herself. We are the Universe living herself, experiencing herself and watching and observing her many manifestations. We bear witness to all that the Universe is, that the divine is, marvel and tremble at her powers, her generosity, her abundance, her terrors. She has allowed us to experience her, allowed us in some way to know her. And how do we do this? Through silent observation, through reverence and consideration of all, through humility at taking part in this great gift of life. Have you ever listened to a bird's song and wondered what it is declaring, who he is singing to? Have you ever watched a snail come out after the rain, her house on her back and wondered why the rain stirs her so, or watched the weeping willow as the wind passes through her and wondered what she felt? Every creature has a story to tell, a journey they have made, a wisdom to share, every creature in the words of Meister Eckhart "a book about God". And as we watch and bear witness to these creatures, perhaps we can learn once again how to be part of nature, how to relate to the other species we share the planet with. Perhaps we can learn to let go of the existential angst that has come to be associated with being human; the rage and frustration that comes with our human limitations. Perhaps we can learn gratitude for the mysterious gift that life is, despite its sufferings and disappointments and brevity. Perhaps we can learn that the divine is fully present in us, present and living on this Earth and beating in our own fragile heart, dependent on our eyes to see her, our ears to hear her and our lives to proclaim and rejoice her. Perhaps then our heart will open up to the mystery and we will realise that our role is to celebrate what is here, was here before us, and will be after us. To praise it and wonder about it and be in awe and gratitude of it.

The Collective Mind

And as we watch we are learning. We are learning about the Universe from the symbols and information and feelings and thoughts and creation that she is unfolding to us, that she is also unfolding within us. Slowly we have learned of her many transformations, her immensity and magnitude, her darkness. We have documented and recorded what we are learning and passed it on so that those who come after us may also add to it. We are helping to build a picture of what this Universe is, a picture that has been changed and modified as we have learnt more, a picture that even as we assemble it, contains us.

All things contain darkness, something inexplicable that often pains us, so it is with the mind that the human is creating. We are yet to learn the full potential of technology or machines, the full potential of what we are creating. And yet, as human beings, create we must and so with or against our will, we are creating a mind fashioned by history and culture, by the sweeping winds and spirit of change, a mind that is stored in books and technology and instruments, and in the human being. And perhaps this is what the human species is here to do, to complete and reflect back what the Universe herself is building. Ever more complex, ever more diverse, ever more spiritual, going somewhere, building something. And maybe that is us, in the same way that it is every creature, but, with the consciousness given us, perhaps it is ours to help unveil the mystery, to make the divine more transparent through description, explanation and representation of her creation.

Chapter 15
Conclusion

This story, the story of the Universe has changed me. It has opened me up to the larger picture of life, married science and spirit, given me hope. Most deeply, it has given me gratitude. I still have no answers and life remains a search but I feel the deeper meaning of things, our connection and interdependency with everything. This story has given me trust - trust in the force that has sustained life on its precarious path to lead us to where we are now and trust in our own human species, even amidst all our destructive tendencies do we not remain as natural a creature as any, are we not one sequence within the Earth's transformative sequences, another manifestation of the Universe?

The human being needs now more than ever, to be reminded of how we came to be, of what we are and of what we could be, of the nature and capabilities inherent in humanity and the potential these have to contribute to the Universe, to enable her to reveal herself through us. We need to be reminded of the great Mystery at the heart of this Universe that is calling us to a destiny that is singularly human, of the spirit that is dancing with us through the tumult of the centuries, through the destruction and the anguish, dancing with us as we take our next step, consciously and tenderly. We need to be reminded of the goodness, compassion and love that form the root of our being, of the spirit within us. We need to be reminded that we are the dreaming species and that it is time for us to dream again, a dream where the human being dreams not just for herself but for the Earth whereon she lives and for all those we share this home with; a dream where the human being is a benevolent part of this planet and no longer a destructive force, a dream where the human being lives to reflect and admire and celebrate a world that is already beautiful.

Notes

Introduction

1. Sagan, C. (1980) *Cosmos.* Random House, NY, 318

What do we know.......A Brief Cosmic History

1. Swimme, Brian & Tucker, Mary Evelyn (2011) *Journey of the Universe.* Yale, 29
2. Fortey, Richard (1997) *Life: An Unauthorised Biography.* Flamingo, U.K, 370
3. Sheldrake, Rupert (2012) Unity and Division in the Sciences in *GreenSpirit Magazine Summer 2012,* 6

Principles of the Universe

1. Holy Names University Reader (2010) *Geo-Wisdom, Cosmology and Human Spirit*, HNU, Oakland, C.A., 25
2. DeGrasse Tyson, Neil (2013) www.haydenplanetarium.org
3. Emerson, Ralph Waldo (1836) *Nature.* Amazon, Marston Gate, England, 25
4. De Chardin, Pierre Teilhard (1999) *The Human Phenomenon,* Appleton-Weber, S (ed.), 3
5. De Chardin, Pierre Teilhard (1999) *The Human Phenomenon,* Appleton-Weber, S (ed.), 17
6. Duncan, T & Tyler, C (2009) *Your Cosmic Context. An Introduction to Modern Cosmology.* Pearson Education Inc., San Francisco, 385
7. Fortey, Richard (1997) *Life: An Unauthorised Biography.* Flamingo, U.K, 32
8. Dellinger, D. (2007). *Love Letter to the Milky Way.* A book of poems. Poets for Global Justice, 30

The Self-Reflective Creature

1. Duncan, T & Tyler, C (2009) *Your Cosmic Context. An Introduction to Modern Cosmology.* Pearson Education Inc., San Francisco, 400
2. Algis Mickunas (1997) An Introduction to the Philosophy of Jean Gebser. *Integrative Explorations Journal,* Vol.4, No.1, 2
3. Ibid.,3

Poverty and Abundance

1. United Nations Development Programme Report (1998), p2

Love

1. De Chardin, Pierre Teilhard (1999) *The Human Phenomenon,* Appleton-Weber, S (ed.), 188
2. Ibid., 189

Communication

1. Mesle, R. (2008) *Process-Relational Philosophy: An Introduction to Alfred North Whitehead*, Templeton Press, P.A., 73
2. Berry, Thomas (2009) *The Sacred Universe*, Columbia Press, NY, 145
3. Barks, Coleman (2005) *Rumi: The book of Love.* HarperCollins, NY , xix
4. Conlon, J (2013) *Sacred Butterflies: Poems, Prayers and Practices.* Wyndham Hall Press, OH., 5
5. Ibid.

Friendship and Joy

1. Wilson, E.O. (2012) *The Social Conquest of Earth*, Liverwright Publishing, N.Y.,193
2. Berry, Thomas. An Essay on Affectivity in Classical Confucian Tradition, 10
3. Thoreau, Henry David (1983) *Walden and Civil Disobedience.* Penguin Classics, 178

Violence and Evil

1. De Chardin, Pierre Teilhard (1999) *The Human Phenomenon,* Appleton-Weber, S (ed.), 36
2. O' Murchu, D. (2008) *Ancestral Grace, Meeting God in Our Human Story.* Orbis Books, NY, 68
3. Berry, T. & Swimme, B. (1992) *The Universe Story.* Harper, San Francisco, 268

Authenticity

1. Cosmos: A Personal Voyage. Series. Produced by PBC 1980
2. Duncan, T & Tyler, C (2009) *Your Cosmic Context. An Introduction to Modern Cosmology.* Pearson Education Inc., San Francisco, 49
3. Berry, Thomas. An Essay on Authenticity in Confucian Spirituality, 2
4. Wilde, Oscar (1997) Collected Works of Oscar Wilde. Wordsworth Editions Ltd., 930
5. Ibid., 954

6. Berry, Thomas (1988) *The Dream of the Earth,* Sierra Club Books, San Francisco, 208

The Meaning of Life to Earth
1. Fortey, Richard (1997) *Life: An Unauthorised Biography.* Flamingo, U.K, 43
2. Dawkins, Richard (2004) *The Ancestor's Tale.* Orion Publishing Group, Great Britain, p.577
3. De Chardin, Pierre Teilhard (1999) *The Human Phenomenon,* Appleton-Weber, S (ed.) p.51
4. Duncan, T & Tyler, C (2009) *Your Cosmic Context. An Introduction to Modern Cosmology.* Pearson Education Inc., San Francisco, 385
5. Abrams, Nancy Ellen & Primack, Joel (2011) *The New Universe and the Human Future,* Yale University Press, p.138
6. Earth from Space website http://www.solarviews.com/eng/earthsp.htm#quote accessed February 6th 2012

Is this the Human Role?
1. De Chardin, Pierre Teilhard (1999) *The Human Phenomenon,* Appleton-Weber, S (ed), 186
2. Rainer Maria Rilke (2008) *Letters to a Young Poet.* BN Publishing, 27
3. Ibid., 37

Bibliography

Abram, D. (1996) *The Spell of the Sensuous.* Random House, NY

Abrams, N. & Primack, J. (2011) *The New Universe and the Human Future*, Yale University Press, New Haven and London

Barks, Coleman (2005) *Rumi: The book of Love*. HarperCollins, NY

Beloff, J. (1994) Minds and Machines: A Radical Dualist Perspective. *Journal of Consciousness Studies,* Vol. 1, No. 1.

Berry, Thomas (1999) *The Great Work*. Bell Tower, N.Y.

Berry, Thomas (2009) *The Sacred Universe*, Columbia Press, NY

Berry, Thomas (1988) *The Dream of the Earth,* Sierra Club Books, San Francisco

Berry, T. & Swimme, B (1992) *The Universe Story*. Harper Collins, N.Y.

Berry, Thomas. An Essay on Authenticity in Confucian Spirituality

Berry, Thomas. An Essay on Affectivity in Classical Confucian Tradition

Bohm, D. (1980) *Wholeness and the Implicate Order*, Routledge, London

Chopra, D. (2003) *The Spontaneous Fulfillment of Desire.* Three Rivers Press, NY,

Coelho, M. *The Depth of Our Belonging to the Unfolding Story*. Talk given at All Saints Parish, Brookline, MA. Oct 18th 2013.

Conlon, J (2011) *Invisible Excursions*. Wyndham Hall Press, OH

Conlon, J (1994) *Earth Story, Sacred Story*. Twenty-third Publications, U.S.A.

Conlon, J. (2007) *From the Stars to the Streets*. Novalis, Canada.

Conlon, J (2013) *Sacred Butterflies: Poems, Prayers and Practices*. Wyndham Hall Press, OH.

Confucius. Confucian Society.

Dawkins, Richard (2004) *The Ancestor's Tale*. Phoenix, London

De Chardin, Pierre Teilhard (1999) *The Human Phenomenon,* Appleton-Weber, S (ed.)

DeGrasse Tyson, Neil (2013) http://www.haydenplanetarium.org/tyson/read (accessed June 27th 2013)

Dellinger, D. (2007). *Love Letter to the Milky Way*. A book of poems. Poets for Global Justice

Dewey, B. (1993) *Consciousness and Quantum Behavior*. Bartholomew Books, CA.,

Duncan, T & Tyler, C (2009) *Your Cosmic Context. An Introduction to Modern Cosmology*. Pearson Education Inc., San Francisco

Emerson, Ralph Waldo.(1836) *Nature*. Amazon, Marston Gate, England

Fortey, Richard (1997) *Life: An Unauthorised Biography*. Flamingo, London

Harman, W. (1994) The Scientific Exploration of Consciousness: Towards an Adequate Epistemology. *Journal of Consciousness Studies,* Vol. 1, No. 1,

Heinrich Boll Foundation. (2002).*The Jo'Burg Memo. Fairness in a Fragile World. Memorandum for the World Summit on Sustainable Development*. World Summit Papers, Special Edition

Holy Names University Reader (2010) *Geo-Wisdom, Cosmology and Human Spirit*, HNU, Oakland, C.A.

House of the Oireachtas, Joint Committee on Health and Children. *The High Level of Suicide in Irish Society. Seventh Report.* July 2006. Available online at www.nosp.ie

King, Ursula (1996) *Spirit of Fire. The Life and Vision of Teilhard de Chardin*. Orbis Books, Maryknoll, NY

Lachman, G. (2010). Jean Gebser, Cartographer of Consciousness. *EnlightenNext Magazine*, Spring/Summer 2010

Mahood, E. (2008) The Primordial Leap and the Present: The Ever-Present Origin – An Overview of the Work of Jean Gebser. www.gaiamind.org/Gebser.html

Mesle, R. (2008) *Process-Relational Philosophy: An Introduction to Alfred North Whitehead*, Templeton Press, P.A.

Morter, G & Brennan, N. (2014) *The Universe Story in Science and Myth*. Greenspirit ebook Series

Mickunas, A. (1997) An Introduction to the Philosophy of Jean Gebser. *Integrative Explorations Journal,* Vol.4, No.1.

Oliver, M. (1992) *New and Selected Poems*, Beacon Press, Boston

O' Murchu, D. (2008) *Ancestral Grace, Meeting God in Our Human Story*. Orbis Books, NY

O'Murchu, D. (2004) *Quantum Theology. Spiritual Implications of the New Physics*. Crossroad Publishing Company, N.Y.

Rainer Maria Rilke (2008) *Letters to a Young Poet.* BN Publishing.

Sachs, Wolfgang (Ed,)(2005) *The Development Dictionary*. Zed Books, London

Sagan, Carl (1983) *Cosmos: The Story of Cosmic Evolution, Science and Civilisation.* Futura

Swimme, B.(1996) *The Hidden Heart of the Cosmos,* Orbis

Swimme, Brian & Tucker, Mary Evelyn (2011) *Journey of the Universe*. Yale

Thoreau, Henry David (1983) *Walden and Civil Disobedience*. Penguin Classics

United Nations Development Statistics (2014) www.un.org

Wilde, Oscar (1997) Collected Works of Oscar Wilde. Wordsworth
    Editions Ltd.,

Wilson, E.O. (2012) *The Social Conquest of Earth*, Liverwright
    Publishing, N.Y.

Wilson, E. O. (2002) *The Future of Life*. Abacus, London

ABOUT THE AUTHOR

Niamh Brennan (MA Development Studies; MA Culture and Spirituality) is a writer and workshop facilitator in the area of cosmology and spirituality. She is co-author with Greg Morter of the e-book *'The Universe Story in Science and Myth'* for Green Spirit. She has contributed to several journals including The Furrow, Spirituality, the IMU Report and the Emmaus website. She has written and presented workshops on 'Advent – A Time of Becoming'; 'Lent – When the Small Self dies into the Larger Self'; 'Darkness, Time and Creativity' and 'Emergent Spirituality in light of our Cosmic Story' all based on the new cosmology. She has worked for a number of years in the Philippines with the Society of St. Columban. She is currently pursuing her Phd on 'The Universe Story in its Theological and Anthropological Reception.'